On Nature

and the Environment

Also by J. Krishnamurti

On Nature
and the Environment

J. Krishnamurti

HarperSanFrancisco
A Division of HarperCollins*Publishers*

For additional information, write to:
Krishnamurti Foundation Trust, Ltd.
Brockwood Park, Bramdean, Hants, England SO24 0LQ

or

Krishnamurti Foundation of America
P.O. Box 1560
Ojai, CA 93023, United States

Sources and acknowledgments can be found on page 113.

Series editor: Mary Cadogan

Associate editors: Ray McCoy and David Skitt

FIRST EDITION

Library of Congress Cataloging-in-Publication Data

Krishnamurti, J. (Jiddu), 1895–1986.

On nature and the environment / J. Krishnamurti. — 1st ed.

p.   cm.

ISBN 0-06-250534-3

1. Philosophy of nature.   2. Philosophy.   3. Life.   I. Title.

B5134.K7530565   1991

113—dc20   90-56457

                                                              CIP

91 92 93 94 95   FAIR   10 9 8 7 6 5 4 3 2 1

This edition is printed on acid-free paper that meets the American
National Standards Institute Z39.48 Standard.

If you lose touch with nature you lose touch with humanity. If there's no relationship with nature then you become a killer; then you kill baby seals, whales, dolphins, and man, either for gain, for "sport," for food, or for knowledge. Then nature is frightened of you, withdrawing its beauty. You may take long walks in the woods or camp in lovely places, but you are a killer and so lose their friendship. You probably are not related to anything, to your wife or your husband.

Krishnamurti's Journal, *4 April 1975*

Contents

Foreword

JIDDU KRISHNAMURTI was born in India in 1895 and, at the age of thirteen, taken up by the Theosophical Society, which considered him to be the vehicle for the "world teacher" whose advent it had been proclaiming. Krishnamurti was soon to emerge as a powerful, uncompromising and unclassifiable teacher, whose talks and writings were not linked to any specific religion and were neither of the East nor the West but for the whole world. Firmly repudiating the messianic image, in 1929 he dramatically dissolved the large and monied organization that had been built around him, and declared truth to be "a pathless land," which could not be approached by any formalized religion, philosophy, or sect.

For the rest of his life he insistently rejected the guru-status that others tried to foist upon him. He continued to attract large audiences throughout the world but claimed no authority, wanted no disciples, and spoke always as one individual to another. At the core of his teaching was the realization that fundamental changes in society can be brought about only by a transformation of individual consciousness. The need for self-knowledge and an understanding of the restrictive, separative influences of religious and nationalistic conditionings, was constantly stressed. Krishnamurti pointed always to the urgent need for openness, for that "vast space in the brain in which there is unimaginable energy." This seems to have been the wellspring of his own creativity and the key to his catalytic impact on such a wide variety of people.

He continued to speak all over the world until he died in 1986 at the age of ninety. His talks and dialogues, journals and letters have been collected into more than sixty books. From that vast body of teachings this series of theme books has been compiled. Each book in the series focuses on an issue that has particular relevance and urgency in our daily lives.

On Nature
and the Environment

Poona, 17 October 1948

Questioner: What is the meaning of right relationship with nature?

Krishnamurti: I do not know if you have discovered your relationship with nature. There is no "right" relationship, there is only the understanding of relationship. Right relationship implies the mere acceptance of a formula, as does right thought. Right thought and right thinking are two different things. Right thought is merely conforming to what is right, what is respectable, whereas right thinking is movement; it is the product of understanding, and understanding is constantly undergoing modification, change. Similarly, there is a difference between right relationship, and understanding our relationship with nature. What is your relationship with nature (nature being the rivers, the trees, the swift-flying birds, the fish in the water, the minerals under the earth, the waterfalls and shallow pools)? What is your relationship to them? Most of us are not aware of that relationship. We never look at a tree, or if we do, it is with a view to using that tree, either to sit in its shade, or to cut it down for lumber. In other words, we look at trees with utilitarian purpose; we never look at a tree without projecting ourselves and utilizing it for our own convenience. We treat the earth and its products in the same way. There is no love of earth, there is only usage of earth. If one really loved the earth, there would be frugality in using the things of the earth. That is, if we were to

understand our relationship with the earth, we should be very careful in the use we made of the things of the earth. The understanding of one's relationship with nature is as difficult as understanding
one's relationship with one's neighbour, wife, and children. But we
have not given a thought to it, we have never sat down to look at
the stars, the moon, or the trees. We are too busy with social or
political activities. Obviously, these activities are escapes from ourselves, and to worship nature is also an escape from ourselves. We
are always using nature, either as an escape or for utilitarian ends—
we never actually stop and love the earth or the things of the earth.
We never enjoy the rich fields, though we utilize them to feed and
clothe ourselves. We never like to till the earth with our hands—
we are ashamed to work with our hands. There is an extraordinary
thing that takes place when you work the earth with your hands.
But this work is done only by the lower castes; we upper classes are
much too important apparently to use our own hands! So, we have
lost our relationship with nature.

If once we understood that relationship, its real significance, then we would not divide property into yours and mine;
though one might own a piece of land and build a house on it, it
would not be "mine" or "yours" in the exclusive sense—it would
be more a means of taking shelter. Because we do not love the
earth and the things of the earth but merely utilize them, we are
insensitive to the beauty of a waterfall, we have lost the touch of
life, we have never sat with our backs against the trunk of a tree.
And since we do not love nature, we do not know how to love
human beings and animals. Go down the street and watch how the
bullocks are treated, their tails all out of shape. You shake your
head and say, "Very sad." But we have lost the sense of tenderness, that sensitivity, that response to things of beauty, and it is
only in the renewal of that sensitivity that we can have understanding of what is true relationship. That sensitivity does not come in
the mere hanging of a few pictures, or in painting a tree, or putting
a few flowers in your hair; sensitivity comes only when this utilitarian outlook is put aside. It does not mean that you cannot use the

earth; but you must use the earth as it is meant to be used. Earth is there to be loved, to be cared for, not to be divided as yours and mine. It is foolish to plant a tree in a compound and call it "mine." It is only when one is free of exclusiveness that there is a possibility of having sensitivity, not only to nature, but to human beings and to the ceaseless challenges of life.

New Delhi, 14 November 1948

WE SEE IN the world about us confusion, misery, and conflicting desires, and, realizing this world chaos, most thoughtful and earnest people—not the people who are playing at make believe, but people who are really concerned—will naturally see the importance of thinking out the problem of action. There is mass action and individual action; and mass action has become an abstraction, a convenient escape for the individual. By thinking that this chaos, this misery, this disaster that is constantly arising can somehow be transformed or brought to order by mass action, the individual becomes irresponsible. The mass is surely a fictitious entity; the mass is you and I. It is only when you and I do not understand the relationship of true action that we turn to the abstraction called the mass—and thereby become irresponsible in our action. For reform in action, we look either to a leader or to organized, collective action, which again is mass action. When we turn to a leader for direction in action, we invariably choose a person we think will help us to go beyond our own problems, our own misery. But, because we choose a leader out of our confusion, the leader himself is also confused. We do not choose a leader unlike ourselves; we cannot. We can only choose a leader who, like ourselves, is confused; therefore, such leaders, such guides and so-called spiritual gurus, invariably lead us to further confusion, to further misery. Since what we choose must be out of our own confusion, when we follow a leader we are only following our own confused self-projection. Therefore, such action, though it may produce an immediate result, invariably leads to further disaster.

So, we see that mass action—though in certain cases worthwhile—is bound to lead to disaster, to confusion, and bring about irresponsibility on the part of the individual, and that the following of a leader must also increase confusion. And yet we have to live. To live, is to act; to be, is to be related. There is no action without relationship, and we cannot live in isolation. There is no such thing as isolation. Life is to act and to be related. So, to understand the action that does not create further misery, further confusion, we have to understand ourselves, with all our contradictions, our opposing elements, our many facets that are constantly in battle with each other. Till we understand ourselves, action must inevitably lead to further conflict, to further misery.

So, our problem is to act with understanding, and that understanding can come about only through self-knowledge. After all, the world is the projection of myself. What I am, the world is; the world is not different from me, the world is not opposed to me. The world and I are not separate entities. Society is myself; there are not two different processes. The world is my own extension, and to understand the world I have to understand myself. The individual is not in opposition to the mass, to society, because society is the individual. Society is the relationship between you and me and another. There is opposition between the individual and society only when the individual becomes irresponsible. So, our problem is considerable. There is an extraordinary crisis that faces every country, every person, every group. What relationship have we, you and I, to that crisis, and how shall we act? Where shall we begin so as to bring about a transformation? As I said, if we look to the mass there is no way out, because the mass implies a leader, and the mass is always exploited by the politician, the priest, and the expert. And since you and I make up the mass, we have to assume the responsibility for our own action, that is, we have to understand our own nature, we have to understand ourselves. To understand ourselves is not to withdraw from the world, because to withdraw implies isolation, and we cannot live in isolation. So, we have to understand action in relationship, and that understanding depends on awareness of our own conflicting and contradictory nature. I think it is foolish to conceive of a state in which there is peace and to which we can look. There can be peace and tranquillity only when we understand the nature of ourselves and not presuppose a state that we do not know. There may be a state of peace, but mere speculation about it is useless.

In order to act rightly, there must be right thinking; to think rightly, there must be self-knowledge; and self-knowledge can come about only through relationship, not through isolation. Right thinking can come only in understanding ourselves, from which there springs right action. Right action is that which comes out of the understanding of ourselves, not one part of ourselves, but the whole content of ourselves, our contradictory natures, all that we are. As we understand ourselves, there is right action, and from that action there is happiness. After all, it is happiness that we want, that most of us are seeking through various forms, through various escapes—the escapes of social activity, of the bureaucratic world, of amusement, of worship and the repetition of phrases, of sex, and innumerable other escapes. But we see these escapes do not bring lasting happiness, they give only a temporary alleviation. Fundamentally, there is nothing true in them, no lasting delight. I think we will find that delight, that ecstasy, that real joy of creative being, only when we understand ourselves. This understanding of ourselves is not easy, it needs a certain alertness, awareness. That alertness, that awareness, can come only when we do not condemn, when we do not justify, because the moment there is condemnation or justification, there is a putting an end to the process of understanding. When we condemn someone, we cease to understand that person, and when we identify ourselves with that person, we again cease to understand him. It is the same with ourselves. To observe, to be passively aware of what you are, is most difficult, but out of that passive awareness there comes an understanding, there comes a transformation of what is, and it is only that transformation that opens the door to reality.

Our problem, then, is action, understanding, and happiness. There is no foundation for true thinking unless we know ourselves. Without knowing myself, I have no foundation for thought—I can only live in a state of contradiction, as most of us do. To bring about a transformation in the world, which is the world of my relationship, I must begin with myself. You may say, "To bring about transformation in the world that way will take an infinitely long time." If we are seeking immediate results, naturally we will think it takes too long. The immediate results are promised by the politicians, but I am afraid for the man seeking truth there is no immediate result. It is truth that transforms, not the immediate action; it is only the discovery of truth by each one that will bring about happiness and peace in the world. To live in the world and yet not be of the world is our problem, and it is a problem of earnest pursuit because we cannot withdraw, we cannot renounce, but we have to understand ourselves. The understanding of oneself is the beginning of wisdom. To understand oneself is to understand one's relationship with things, people, and ideas. Until we understand the full significance and meaning of our relationship with things, people, and ideas, action, which is relationship, will inevitably bring about conflict and strife. So a man who is really earnest must begin with himself; he must be passively aware of all his thoughts, feelings, and actions. Again, this is not a matter of time. There is no end to self-knowledge. Self-knowledge is only from moment to moment, and therefore there is a creative happiness from moment to moment.

❖

WHEN I DEAL with your questions, please do not wait for an answer; because you and I are going to think out the problem together and find the answer in the problem. If you merely wait for an answer, I am afraid you will be disappointed. Life has no categorical "yes" or "no" although that is what we would like. Life is more complex than that, more subtle. So, to find the answer we must study the problem, which means we must have the patience and intelligence to go into it.

Questioner: What place has organized religion in modern society?

Krishnamurti: Let us find out what we mean by religion and what we mean by modern society. What do we mean by religion? What does religion mean to you? It means, does it not, a set of beliefs; ritual; dogmas; many superstitions; puja; the repetition of words; vague, unfulfilled, frustrated hopes; reading certain books; pursuing gurus; going to the temple occasionally; and so on. Surely, all that is religion to most of our people. But is that religion? Is religion a custom, a habit, a tradition? Surely, religion is something far beyond all that, is it not? Religion implies the search for reality, which has nothing whatever to do with organized belief, temples, dogmas, or rituals, and yet our thinking, the very fabric of our being, is enmeshed, caught up in beliefs, superstitions, and so on. Obviously, modern man is not religious; therefore, his society is not a sane, balanced society. We may follow certain doctrines, worship certain pictures, or create a new religion of the State, but obviously, all these things are not religion. I said that religion is the search for reality, but that reality is unknown; it is not the reality of the books; it is not the experience of others. To find that reality, to uncover it, to invite it, the known must stop; the significance of all the traditions and beliefs must be gone into, understood, and discarded. For this, the repetition of rituals has no meaning. So a man who is religious obviously does not belong to any religion, to any organization; he is neither Hindu nor Moslem; he does not belong to any class.

Now, what is the modern world? The modern world is made up of technique and efficiency in mass organizations. There is an extraordinary advancement in technology and a maldistribution of mass needs; the means of production are in the hands of a few. There are conflicting nationalities, constantly recurring wars because of sovereign governments, and so on. That is the modern world, is it not? There is technical advancement without an equally vital psychological advancement, and so there is a state of unbalance; there are extraordinary scientific achievements, and at the same time human misery, empty hearts, and empty minds. Many of the techniques we have learned have to do with building airplanes, killing each other, and so on. So that is the modern world, which is yourself. The world is not different from you. Your world, which is yourself, is a world of the cultivated intellect and the empty heart. If you look into yourselves, you will see that you are the very product of modern civilization. You know how to do a few tricks, technical, physical tricks, but you are not creative human beings. You produce children, but that is not creative. To be able to create, one needs extraordinary inward richness, and that richness can come about only when we understand truth, when we are capable of receiving truth.

So organized religion and the modern world go together; they both cultivate the empty heart, and that is the unfortunate part of our existence. We are superficial, intellectually brilliant, capable of great inventions and of producing the most destructive means of liquidating each other, and creating more and more division between ourselves. But we do not know what it means to love; we have no song in our hearts. We play music, listen to the radio, but there is no singing, because our hearts are empty. We have created a world that is utterly confused, miserable, and our relationships are flimsy, superficial. Yes, organized religion and the modern world go together, because both lead to confusion, and this confusion of organized religion and the modern world is the outcome of ourselves. They are the self-projected expressions of ourselves. So there can be no transformation in the world outside unless there is a transformation within the skin of each one of us, and to bring about that transformation is not the problem of the expert, of the specialist, of the leader, or the priest. It is the problem of each one of us. If we leave it to others, we become irresponsible, and therefore our hearts become empty. An empty heart with a technical mind is not a creative human being, and because we have lost that creative state, we have produced a world that is utterly miserable, confused, broken by wars, torn by class and racial distinctions. It is our responsibility to bring about a radical transformation within ourselves.

From From Darkness to Light

Listen!

Life is one.
It has no beginning, no end,
The source and the goal live in your heart.
You are caught up
In the darkness of its wide chasm.

Life has no creed, no belief,
It is of no nation, of no sanctuary,
Not bound by birth or by death,
Neither male nor female.
Can you bind the "waters in a garment"
Or "gather the wind in your fists?"

Answer, O friend.

Drink at the fountain of Life.
Come,
I will show the way.
The mantle of Life covers all things.

From Krishnamurti's Journal, *6 April 1975*

IT IS NOT that extraordinary blue of the Mediterranean; the Pacific has an ethereal blue, especially when there is a gentle breeze from the west as you drive north along the coast road. It is so tender, dazzling, clear, and full of mirth. Occasionally you would see whales blowing on their way north and, rarely, their enormous heads as they threw themselves out of the water. There was a whole pod of them, blowing; they must be very powerful animals. That day the sea was a lake, still and utterly quiet, without a single wave; there was not that clear dancing blue. The sea was asleep and you watched it with wonder. The house overlooked the sea. [This is the house where he was staying in Malibu.] It is a beautiful house, with a quiet garden, a green lawn, and flowers. It's a spacious house with the light of the California sun. And rabbits loved it too; they would come early in the morning and late in the evening; they would eat up flowers and the newly planted pansies, marigolds, and the small flowering plants. You couldn't keep them out though there was a wire netting all around, and to kill them would be a crime. But a cat and a barn owl brought order to the garden; the black cat wandered about the garden; the owl perched itself during the day among the thick eucalyptus. You could see it, motionless, eyes closed, round and big. The rabbits disappeared and the garden flourished and the blue Pacific flowed effortlessly.

It is only man that brings disorder to the universe. He's ruthless and extremely violent. Wherever he is he brings misery and confusion in himself and in the world about him. He lays waste and destroys, and he has no compassion. In himself there is no order, and so what he touches becomes soiled and chaotic. His politics have become a refined gangsterism of power, deceit, personal or national, group against group. His economy is restricted and so not universal. His society is immoral, in freedom and under tyranny. He is not religious though he believes, worships, and goes through endless, meaningless rituals. Why has he become like this—cruel, irresponsible, and so utterly self-centred? Why? There are a hundred explanations and those who explain, subtly with words that are born out of knowledge of many books and experiments on animals, are caught in the net of human sorrow, ambition, pride, and agony. The description is not the described; the word is not the thing. Is it because he is looking for outward causes, the environment conditioning man, hoping the outer change transforms the inner man? Is it because he's so attached to his senses, dominated by their immediate demands? Is it because he lives so entirely in the movement of thought and knowledge? Or is it because he's so romantic, sentimental, that he becomes ruthless with his ideals, make-beliefs, and pretensions? Is it because he is always led, a follower, or becomes a leader, a guru?

This division as the outer and inner is the beginning of his conflict and misery; he is caught in this contradiction, in this ageless tradition. Caught in this meaningless division, he is lost and becomes a slave to others. The outer and the inner are imagination and the invention of thought; as thought is fragmentary, it makes for disorder and conflict, which is division. Thought cannot bring about order, an effortless flow of virtue. Virtue is not the continuous repetition of memory, practice. Thought-knowledge is time binding. Thought by its very nature and structure cannot grasp the whole flow of life, as a total movement. Thought-knowledge cannot have an insight into this wholeness; it cannot be aware of this choicelessly as long as it remains as the perceiver, the outsider looking in. Thought-knowledge has no place in perception. The thinker is the thought; the perceiver is the perceived. Only then is there an effortless movement in our daily life.

New Delhi, 28 November 1948

IT SEEMS TO ME that it is important to understand that conflict of any kind does not produce creative thinking. Until we understand conflict and the nature of conflict, and what it is that one is in conflict with, merely to struggle with a problem, or with a particular background or environment, is utterly useless. Just as all wars create deterioration and inevitably produce further wars, further misery, so too struggle with conflict leads to further confusion. So, conflict within oneself, projected outwardly, creates confusion in the world. It is therefore necessary, is it not, to understand conflict and to see that conflict of any kind is not productive of creative thinking, of sane human beings. And yet all our life is spent in struggle, and we think that struggle is a necessary part of existence. There is conflict within oneself and with the environment, environment being society, which in turn is our relationship with people, with things, and with ideas. This struggle is considered as inevitable, and we think that struggle is essential for the process of existence. Now, is that so? Is there any way of living that excludes struggle, in which there is a possibility of understanding without the usual conflict? I do not know whether you have noticed that the more you struggle with a psychological problem, the more confused and entangled you get, and that it is only when there is cessation of struggle, of all thought process, that understanding comes.

So, we will have to inquire if conflict is essential, and if conflict is productive.

Now, we are talking about conflict in ourselves and with the environment. The environment is what one is in oneself. You and the environment are not two different processes; you are the environment, and the environment is you—which is an obvious fact. You are born into a particular group of people, whether in India, America, Russia, or England, and that very environment with its influences of climate, tradition, social and religious custom, creates you—and you are that environment. To find out if there is something more than merely the result of environment, you have to be free of the environment, free of its conditioning. That is obvious, is it not? If you look carefully into yourself, you will see that, being born in this country, you are climatically, socially, religiously, and economically its product or result. That is, you are conditioned. To find out if there is something more, something greater than the mere result of a condition, you have to be free of that condition. Being conditioned, merely to inquire if there is something more, something greater than the mere product of environment, has no meaning. Obviously, we must be free of the condition, of the environment, and then only can we find out if there is something more. To assert that there is or is not something more, is surely a wrong way of thinking. One has to discover, and to discover, one has to experiment.

❖

SO, IN CONSIDERING these questions, please let us bear in mind that we are undertaking a journey together to discover things together; therefore, there is no danger of the relationship of pupil and teacher. You are not here as the spectator to watch me play; we are both playing, therefore neither of us is exploiting the other.

Varanasi, 22 November 1964

IF YOU ARE NOT in communion with anything, you are a dead human being. You have to be in communion with the river, with the birds, with the trees, with the extraordinary light of the evening, the light of the morning on the water; you have to be in communion with your neighbour, with your wife, with your children, with your husband. I mean by *communion* non-interference of the past, so that you look at everything afresh, anew—and that's the only way to be in communion with something, so that you die to everything of yesterday. And is it possible? One has to find this out, not ask "How am I to do it?"—that is such an idiotic question. People always ask, "How am I to do this?" This shows their mentality; they have not understood, but they only want to achieve a result.

So I am asking you if you are ever in contact with anything, and if you are ever in contact with yourself—not with your higher self and lower self and all the innumerable divisions that man has created to escape from the fact. And you have to find out—not be told how to come to this total action. There is no "how," there is no method, there is no system; you cannot be told. You have to work for it. I am sorry. I don't mean that word *work;* people love to work; that is one of our fantasies—that we must work to achieve something. You can't work; when you are in a state of communion, there is no working, it is there; the perfume is there, you don't have to work.

So ask yourself, if I may request you, to find out for yourself whether you are in communion with anything—whether you are in communion with a tree. Have you ever been in communion with a tree? Do you know what it means to look at a tree, to have no thought, no memory interfering with your observation, with your feeling, with your sensibility, with your nervous state of attention, so that there is only the tree, not you who are looking at that tree? Probably you have never done this, because for you a tree has no meaning. The beauty of a tree has no significance at all, for to you beauty means sexuality. So you have shut out the tree, nature, the river, the people. And you are not in contact with anything, even with yourself. You are in contact with your own ideas, with your own words, like a human being in contact with ashes. You know what happens when you are in contact with ashes? You are dead; you are burnt out.

So the first thing you have to realize is that you must find out what the total action is that will not create contradiction at any level of your existence, what it is to be in communion, communion with yourself, not with the higher self, not with the Atman, god, and all that, but to be actually in contact with yourself, with your greed, envy, ambition, brutality, deception, and then from there move. Then you will find out for yourself—find out, not be told, which has no meaning—that there is a total action only when there is complete silence of the mind from which there is action.

You know, in the case of most of us, the mind is noisy, everlastingly chattering to itself, soliloquizing or chattering about something, or trying to talk to itself, to convince itself of something; it is always moving, noisy. And from that noise, we act. Any action born of noise produces more noise, more confusion. But if you have observed and learned what it means to communicate, the difficulty of communication, the non-verbalization of the mind— that it is that which communicates and receives communication— then, as life is a movement, you will, in your action, move on naturally, freely, easily, without any effort, to that state of communion. And in that state of communion—if you inquire more deeply—you will find that you are not only in communion with nature, with the world, with everything about you, but also in communion with yourself.

To be in communion with yourself means complete silence, so that the mind can be silently in communion with itself about everything. And from there, there is a total action. It is only out of emptiness that there is the action that is total and creative.

Varanasi, 28 November 1964

ACCORDING TO RECENT discoveries of the anthropologists, man has apparently been living on this earth for about two million years. And man has left in caves, for about seventeen thousand years, records of the struggle, the battle, the unending sorrow of existence—the battle between good and evil, between brutality and the thing he seeks everlastingly: love. And apparently man has not solved his problems—not mathematical problems, not scientific or engineering problems, but human problems of relationship, how to live in this world peaceably, how to be in intimate contact with nature and see the beauty of a bird on a naked branch.

Coming down to modern times, our problems, human problems, are increasing more and more; these problems we try to resolve, according to certain patterns of morality, behaviour, and according to the various commitments that we have given our minds to. According to our commitments, patterns of behaviour, religious formulas and sanctions, we try to solve our problems, our agonies, our despair, our inconstancy, and the contradictions of our lives. We take up a certain attitude as a Communist, a Socialist, this or that; and from that attitude, from that platform as it were, we try to solve our problems piecemeal, one after the other—this is what we do in our lives.

One may be a great scientist, but that very scientist in his laboratory is entirely different from the scientist at home, who is a national, who is bitter, angry, jealous, envious, competitive with his fellow-scientists for a greater name, for greater popularity, and for more money. He is not concerned with human problems at all; he is concerned with the discovery of various forms of matter and the truth of all that.

And we too, being ordinary human beings, not experts, not specialists along any particular line, are committed to a certain pattern of behaviour, to certain religious concepts, or to national poison, and from that we strive to solve the ever increasing, multiplying problems.

You know there is no end to talking, no end to reading. Words can be piled upon words, and the phrasing, the beauty of the language, the reason or the illogicality of what is being said either persuades you or dissuades you. But what is important is not the piling up of words, listening to talks and discourses and reading, but rather resolving the problem—the human problem, your problem—not piecemeal, not as it arises, not according to circumstances, not according to the pressures and strains of modern existence, but from a totally different activity. There are the human problems of greed, envy, the dull spirit of the mind, the aching heart, the appalling insensitivity of man, the brutality, the violence, the deep despair and agony. And during the two million years we have lived, we have tried to solve these problems according to different formulas, different systems, different methods, different gurus, different ways of looking, asking, questioning. And yet we are where we are, caught in this endless process of agony, confusion, and endless despair.

Is there a way of resolving the problems entirely, completely, so that they never arise, and if they do arise, we can meet them instantly and resolve them, dissipate them, put them away? Is there a total way of life that gives no soil to problems; is there a way of living—not the pattern of a way, of a method, of a system, but a total way of living—so that no problem at any time will arise, and if it does arise, can be resolved instantly? A mind that carries the burden of problems becomes a dull, heavy, stupid mind. I do not know if you have watched your own mind and the minds of your wives, husbands, and neighbours. When the mind has problems of any kind, those very problems—even mathematical problems, however complex, however painful, however intriguing, intellectual—make the mind dull. By the word *problem* I mean a difficult question, a difficult relationship, a difficult issue that remains unresolved, and that is carried from day to day. So we are asking if there is a way of living, if there is a state of mind that, because it understands the totality of existence, has no problem, and that, when a problem does arise, can resolve it immediately. Because the moment a problem is carried over even for a day, even for a minute, it makes the mind heavy, dull, and the mind has no sensitivity to look, to observe.

Is there a total action, a state of mind that resolves every problem as it arises, and has no problem in itself, at whatever depth, conscious or unconscious? I do not know if you have ever asked that question of yourself. Probably not, because most of us are so sunk, so held in the problems of everyday existence—earning a livelihood and responding to the demands of a society that psychologically builds a structure of ambition, greed, acquisitiveness—that we have no time to inquire. This morning we are going to inquire into this, and it depends upon you how deeply you inquire, how earnestly you demand, with what clarity and intensity you observe.

We have apparently lived for two million years—a terrible idea! And probably, as human beings are, we shall live another two million years, caught in the everlasting pain of existence. Is there a way, is there something that will free man from this, entirely, so that he will not live even a second in agony, will not invent a philosophy that satisfies him in his agony, will not have a formula that he applies to all the problems that arise, thereby increasing those problems? There is! There is a state of mind that can resolve problems immediately, and therefore, the mind, itself, has no problem, conscious or unconscious.

And we are going to inquire into that. And though the speaker is going to use words and penetrate as far as possible through the communication of words you have to listen and understand. You are a human being, not an individual, because you are still the world, the mass; you are part of this terrible structure of society. There is individuality only when there is a state of mind when the mind has no problems, when it has completely extricated itself from the social structure of acquisitiveness, greed, ambition.

We say that there is a state of mind that can live without any problem and can resolve instantly any problem that arises. You have to see how important it is not to carry a problem over, even for a day or for a second. Because the more you have a problem unresolved, the more you give it soil in which it can take root, the more the mind, the heart, the nervous sensitivity, is destroyed. So it is imperative that the problem should be resolved immediately.

Is it possible, after having lived for two million years with the conflicts, the misery, the remembrance of many yesterdays—is it possible for the mind to free itself from that, so that it is complete, whole, not broken up? And to find that out, one has to inquire into time, because problems and time are closely related.

So we are going to inquire into time. That is, after having lived for two million years, must we go on living another two million years, in sorrow, pain, anxiety, everlasting struggle, death? Is that inevitable? Society is progressing, is evolving that way—evolving through war, through pressure, through this battle of East and West, through the various contentions of nationality, the Common Market, the blocks of this power and that power. Society is moving, moving, moving—slowly, in a sense asleep, but it is moving. Well, perhaps in two million years, society will come to some kind of state where it can live with another human being without competition, with love, with gentleness, with quiet, with an exquisite sense of beauty. But must one wait two million years to come to that? Must one not be impatient? I am using the word *impatient* in the right sense: being impatient, having no patience with time. That is, can we not resolve everything, not in terms of time but immediately?

Do think about this. Do not say it is not possible or it is possible. What is time? There is chronological time, time by the watch—that is obvious, that is necessary; when you have to build a bridge, you have to have time. But every other form of time—that is, "I will be," "I will do," "I must not"—is not true; it is just an invention of a mind that says, "I will do it." If there is no tomorrow—and there is no tomorrow—then your whole attitude is different. And actually there is no such time—when you are hungry, sexual, or lustful, you have no time; you want that thing immediately. So the understanding of time is the resolution of problems.

Please see the intimate relationship between the problem and time. For instance, there is sorrow. You know what sorrow is—not the supreme sorrow, but the sorrow of being lonely, the sorrow of not achieving something you want, the sorrow of not seeing clearly, the sorrow of frustration, the sorrow of having lost somebody whom you think you love, the sorrow of seeing something very clearly, intellectually, and not being able to do it. And beyond this sorrow, there is a still greater sorrow: the sorrow of time. Because it is time that breeds sorrow. Do please listen to this. We have accepted time, which is the gradual process of life, the gradual way of evolving, the gradual change from this to that, from anger to a state of non-anger gradually. We have accepted the gradual process of evolution, and we say that is part of existence, that is part of life, that is god's plan, or the Communist plan, or some other plan. We have accepted it, and we live with that not ideationally, but actually.

Now, for me, that is the greatest sorrow: to allow time to dictate the change, the mutation. Have I to wait ten thousand years and more, have I to go through this misery, conflict, for another ten thousand years, and slowly, gradually change little bit by little bit, take my time, move slowly? To accept that and to live in that state is the greatest sorrow.

❖

Is it possible to end that sorrow immediately? That is the real crux of the matter. Because once I resolve sorrow—sorrow in the deeper sense of that word—everything is over. Because a mind in sorrow can never know what it means to love.

❖

So I have to learn about sorrow immediately, and the very act of learning is the complete cutting away of time. To see something immediately, to see the false immediately—that very seeing of the false is the action of truth that frees you from time.

I am going a little bit into this question of seeing. As we came in just now, there was a parrot: green, bright, with its red beak, on a dead branch against the blue sky. We do not see it at all; we are too occupied, we are too concentrated, we are disturbed, so we never see the beauty of that bird on the dead branch against the blue sky. The act of seeing is immediate—not "I will learn how to see." If you say, "I will learn," you have already introduced time. So, not only to see that bird but also to hear that train, to hear the coughing, this nervous coughing that is going on all the time here—to hear that noise, to listen to it is an immediate act. And it is an immediate act to see very clearly, without the thinker—to see that bird, to see what one is, actually, not the theories about Super Atman and all the rest of it, but to see actually what one is.

To see implies a mind that has no opinion, that has no formula. If you have a formula in your mind, you will never see that bird—that parrot on that branch against the sky—you will never see the total beauty of it. You will say, "Yes, that is a parrot of such and such a species, and the dead branch is of such and such a tree, and the blue of the sky is blue because of light, specks of dirt," but you will never see the totality of that extraordinary thing. And to perceive the totality of that beauty, there is no time. In the same way, to see the totality of sorrow, time must not come in at all.

❖

PLEASE LOOK AT it in another way. You know, actually we have no love—that is a terrible thing to realize. Actually we have no love; we have sentiment; we have emotionality, sensuality, sexuality; we have remembrances of something that we have thought of as love. But actually, brutally, we have no love. Because to have love means no violence, no fear, no competition, no ambition. If you had love you would never say, "This is my family." You may have a family and give them the best you can, but it will not be "your family," which is opposed to the world. If you love, if there is love, there is peace. If you loved, you would educate your child not to be a nationalist, not to have only a technical job and look after his own petty little affairs; you would have no nationality. There would be no divisions of religion, if you loved. But as these things actually exist—not theoretically, but brutally—in this ugly world, it shows that you have no love. Even the love of a mother for her child is not love. If the mother really loved her child, do you think the world would be like this? She would see that he had the right food, the right education, that he was sensitive, that he appreciated beauty, that he was not ambitious, greedy, envious. So the mother, however much she may think she loves her child, does not love the child.

So we have not that love.

❖

SO WHAT WILL you do? If you say, "Please tell me what to do," then you are missing the bus entirely. But you have to see the importance, the immensity, the urgency of that question—not tomorrow, not the next day or the next hour, but see it now. And to see that, you must have energy. So just see immediately—the catalyst that makes the liquid into solid or vaporizes it immediately does not take place if you allow time, even a second. All our existence, all our books, all our hope is tomorrow, tomorrow, tomorrow. This admittance of time is the greatest sorrow.

So the issue is with you, not with the speaker from whom you are expecting to get the answer. There is no answer. That is the beauty of it. You can sit cross-legged, breathe rightly, or stand on your head for the next ten thousand years. Unless you have put this question to yourself—not superficially, not verbally, not intellectually, but with your whole being—you will live with it for two million years. Those two million years may be only tomorrow. So problems and time are intimately related—do you see it now?

❖

A MIND THAT demands an answer to this question has not only to understand that it is the result of time, but also to deny itself, so that it can be outside the structure of time, of society. If you have listened, really listened with urgency, with intensity, you will have come into this—not only verbally, but actually—that you are no longer held in the clutches of time. The mind, though it is the result of two million or more years, is out, because it has seen the whole process and understood it immediately. Up to this one can come—that is fairly obvious. When one sees this thing, that is child's play. Though you are all grown-up people, the moment you see it, you say, "What have I been doing with my life!" Then the mind has no deception, has no pressures.

When the mind has no problems, no tensions, no direction, then such a mind has space, an infinite space both in the mind and in the heart, and it is only in that infinite space that there can be creation. Because sorrow, love, death, and creation are the substance of this mind, this mind is free of sorrow, is free of time. And so this mind is in a state of love, and when there is love, there is beauty. In that sense of beauty, in that sense of vast, infinite space, there is creation. And still further—further not in the sense of time—there is a sense of vast movement.

Now you are all listening to it, hoping to capture it verbally, but you won't—any more than you can capture love by listening to a talk about love. To understand love, you must begin very near, which is yourself. And then when you understand, when you take the first step—and that very first step is also the last step—then you can go very far, much further than the rockets to the moon or to Venus or to Mars. The whole of this is the religious mind.

From Commentaries on Living, Second Series

THE PLANE WAS crowded. It was flying at twenty-odd thousand feet over the Atlantic and there was a thick carpet of clouds below. The sky above was intensely blue, the sun was behind us, and we were flying due west. The children had been playing, running up and down the aisle, and now, tired out, they were sleeping. After the long night everyone else was awake, smoking and drinking. A man in front was telling another about his business, and a woman in the seat behind was describing in a pleased voice the things she had bought and speculating on the amount of duty she would have to pay. At that altitude the flight was smooth, there wasn't a bump, though there were rough winds below us. The wings of the plane were bright in the clear sunlight and the propellers were turning over smoothly, biting into the air at fantastic speed; the wind was behind us and we were doing over three hundred miles an hour.

Two men just across the narrow aisle were talking rather loudly, and it was difficult not to overhear what they were saying. They were big men, and one had a red, weather-beaten face. He was explaining the business of killing whales, how risky it was, what profits there were in it, and how frightfully rough the seas were. Some whales weighed hundreds of tons. The mothers with calves were not supposed to be killed, nor were they permitted to kill more than a certain number of whales within a specified time. Killing these great monsters had apparently been worked out most scientifically, each group having a special job to do for which it was technically trained. The smell of the factory ship was almost unbearable, but one got used to it, as one can to almost anything. But there was lots of money in it if all went well. He began to explain the strange fascination of killing, but at that moment drinks were brought and the subject of conversation changed.

Human beings like to kill, whether it be each other, or a harmless, bright-eyed deer in the deep forest, or a tiger that has preyed upon cattle. A snake is deliberately run over on the road; a trap is set and a wolf or a coyote is caught. Well dressed, laughing people go out with their precious guns and kill birds that were lately calling to each other. A boy kills a chattering blue jay with his air gun, and the elders around him say never a word of pity, or scold him; on the contrary, they say what a good shot he is. Killing for so-called sport, for food, for one's country, for peace—there is not much difference in all this. Justification is not the answer. There is only: do not kill. In the West we think that animals exist for the sake of our stomachs, or for the pleasure of killing, or for their fur. In the East it has been taught for centuries and repeated by every parent: do not kill, be pitiful, be compassionate. Here, animals have no souls, so they can be killed with impunity; there, animals have souls, so consider and let your heart know love. To eat animals, birds, is regarded here as a normal, natural thing, sanctioned by church and advertisements; there, it is not, and the thoughtful, the religious, by tradition and culture, never do. But this too is rapidly breaking down. Here, we have always killed in the name of god and country, and now it is everywhere. Killing is spreading; almost overnight the ancient cultures are being swept aside, and efficiency, ruthlessness, and the means of destruction are being carefully nurtured and strengthened.

Peace is not with the politician or the priest, neither is it with the lawyer or the policeman. Peace is a state of mind when there is love.

From The First and Last Freedom, *Chapter 3*

WHAT IS THE relationship between yourself and the misery, the confusion, in and around you? Surely this confusion, this misery, did not come into being by itself. You and I, not a capitalist nor a communist nor a fascist society have created it, but you and I have created it in our relationship with each other. What you are within has been projected without, onto the world; what you are, what you think and what you feel, what you do in your everyday existence, is projected outwardly, and that constitutes the world. If we are miserable, confused, chaotic within, by projection that becomes the world, that becomes society, because the relationship between yourself and myself, between myself and another, is society—society is the product of our relationship—and if our relationship is confused, egocentric, narrow, limited, national, we project that and bring chaos into the world.

What you are, the world is. So your problem is the world's problem. Surely, this is a simple and basic fact, is it not?

❖

WHY IS SOCIETY crumbling, collapsing, as it surely is? One of the fundamental reasons is that the individual, you, has ceased to be creative. I will explain what I mean. You and I have become imitative; we are copying, outwardly and inwardly. Outwardly, when learning a technique, when communicating with each other on the verbal level, naturally there must be some imitation, copy. I copy words. To become an engineer, I must first learn the technique, then use the technique to build a bridge. There must be a certain amount of imitation, copying, in outward technique, but when there is inward, psychological imitation, surely we cease to be creative. Our education, our social structure, our so-called religious life, are all based on imitation; that is, I fit into a particular social or religious formula. I have ceased to be a real individual. Psychologically, I have become a mere repetitive machine with certain conditioned responses, whether those of the Hindu, the Christian, the Buddhist, the German, or the Englishman. Our responses are conditioned according to the pattern of society, whether it is eastern or western, religious or materialistic. So one of the fundamental causes of the disintegration of society is imitation, and one of the disintegrating factors is the leader, whose very essence is imitation.

From Freedom from the Known, *Chapter 11*

WE HAVE BEEN inquiring into the nature of love and have come to a point, I think, that needs much greater penetration, a much greater awareness of the issue. We have discovered that for most people love means comfort, security, a guarantee for the rest of their lives of continuous emotional satisfaction. Then someone like me comes along and asks, "Is that really love?" and asks you to look inside yourself. And you try not to look because it is very disturbing—you would rather discuss the soul or the political or economic situation—but when you are driven into a corner to look, you realize that what you have always thought of as love is not love at all; it is a mutual gratification, a mutual exploitation.

When I say, "Love has no tomorrow and no yesterday," or, "When there is no centre, then there is love," it has reality for me but not for you. You may quote it and make it into a formula, but that has no validity. You have to see it for yourself, but to do so there must be freedom to look, freedom from all condemnation, all judgment, all agreeing or disagreeing.

Now, to look—or to listen—is one of the most difficult things in life; to look and listen are the same. If your eyes are blinded with your worries, you cannot see the beauty of the sunset. Most of us have lost touch with nature. Civilization is tending more and more toward large cities. We are becoming more and more an urban people, living in crowded apartments and having very little space even to look at the sky of an evening and morning, and therefore we are losing touch with a great deal of beauty. I don't know if you have noticed how few of us look at a sunrise or a sunset or the moonlight or the reflection of light on water.

Having lost touch with nature we naturally tend to develop intellectual capacities. We read a great many books, go to a great many museums and concerts, watch television, and have many other entertainments. We quote endlessly from other people's ideas and think and talk a great deal about art. Why is it that we depend so much upon art? Is it a form of escape, of stimulation? If you are directly in contact with nature, if you watch the movement of a bird on the wing, see the beauty of every movement of the sky, watch the shadows on the hills or the beauty on the face of another, do you think you will want to go to any museum to look at any picture? Perhaps it is because you do not know how to look at all the things about you that you resort to some form of drug to stimulate you to see better.

There is a story of a religious teacher who used to talk every morning to his disciples. One morning he got on to the platform and was just about to begin when a little bird came and sat on the window sill and began to sing, and sang away with full heart. Then it stopped and flew away and the teacher said, "The sermon for this morning is over."

It seems to me that one of our greatest difficulties is to see for ourselves really clearly, not only outward things but inward life. When we say we see a tree or a flower or a person, do we actually see them? Or do we merely see the image that the word has created? That is, when you look at a tree or at a cloud of an evening full of light and delight, do you actually see it, not only with your eyes and intellectually, but totally, completely?

Have you ever experimented with looking at an objective thing such as a tree without any of the associations, any of the knowledge you have acquired about it, without any prejudice, any judgment, any words forming a screen between you and the tree and preventing you from seeing it as it actually is? Try it and see what actually takes place when you observe the tree with all your being, with the totality of your energy. In that intensity you will find that there is no observer at all, there is only attention. It is when there is inattention that there is the observer and the observed. When you are looking at something with complete attention there is no space for a conception, a formula, or a memory. This is important to understand because we are going into something that requires very careful investigation.

It is only a mind that looks at a tree or the stars or the sparkling waters of a river with complete self-abandonment that knows what beauty is, and when we are actually seeing we are in a state of love. We generally know beauty through comparison or through what man has put together, which means that we attribute beauty to some object. I see what I consider to be a beautiful building, and that beauty I appreciate because of my knowledge of architecture and by comparing it with other buildings I have seen. But now I am asking myself, "Is there a beauty without object?" When there is an observer who is the censor, the experiencer, the thinker, there is no beauty because beauty is something external, something the observer looks at and judges. But when there is no observer—and this demands a great deal of meditation, of inquiry—then there is beauty without the object.

Beauty lies in the total abandonment of the observer and the observed, and there can be self-abandonment only when there is total austerity—not the austerity of the priest with its harshness, its sanctions, rules, and obedience, not austerity in clothes, ideas, food and behaviour—but the austerity of being totally simple, which is complete humility. Then there is no achieving, no ladder to climb; there is only the first step, and the first step is the everlasting step.

Say you are walking by yourself or with somebody and you have stopped talking. You are surrounded by nature and there is no dog barking, no noise of a car passing, or even the flutter of a bird.

You are completely silent and nature around you is also wholly silent. In that state of silence both in the observer and the observed—when the observer is not translating what he observes into thought—in that silence there is a different quality of beauty. There is neither nature nor the observer. There is a state of mind wholly, completely, alone; it is alone, not in isolation, but in stillness, and that stillness is beauty. When you love, is there an observer? There is an observer only when love is desire and pleasure. When desire and pleasure are not associated with love, then love is intense. It is, like beauty, something totally new every day. As I have said, it has no today and no tomorrow.

It is only when we see without any preconception, any image, that we are able to be in direct contact with anything in life. All our relationships are really imaginary—that is, based on an image formed by thought. If I have an image about you and you have an image about me, naturally we don't see each other at all as we actually are. What we see is the images we have formed about each other that prevent us from being in contact, and that is why our relationships go wrong.

When I say I know you, I mean I knew you yesterday. I do not know you actually now. All I know is my image of you. That image is put together by what you have said in praise of me or to insult me, what you have done to me; it is put together by all the memories I have of you. And your image of me is put together in the same way, and it is those images that have relationship and that prevent us from really communing with each other.

Two people who have lived together for a long time have an image of each other that prevents them from really being in relationship. If we understand relationship we can co-operate, but co-operation cannot possibly exist through images, through symbols, through ideological conceptions. Only when we understand the true relationship between each other is there a possibility of love, and love is denied when we have images. Therefore it is important to understand, not intellectually but actually in your daily life, how you have built images about your wife, your husband, your neighbour, your child, your country, your leaders, your politicians, your gods—you have nothing but images.

These images create the space between you and what you observe, and in that space there is conflict. So what we are going to find out now together is whether it is possible to be free of the space we create, not only outside ourselves but in ourselves, the space that divides people in all their relationships.

Now the very attention you give to a problem is the energy that solves that problem. When you give your complete attention—I mean with everything in you—there is no observer at all. There is only the state of attention that is total energy, and that total energy is the highest form of intelligence. Naturally that state of mind must be completely silent and that silence, that stillness, comes when there is total attention, not disciplined stillness. That total silence in which there is neither the observer nor the thing observed is the highest form of a religious mind. But what takes place in that state cannot be put into words because what is said in words is not the fact. To find out for yourself you have to go through it.

Every problem is related to every other problem so that if you can solve one problem completely—it does not matter what it is—you will see that you are able to meet all other problems easily and resolve them. We are talking, of course, of psychological problems. We have already seen that a problem exists only in time, that is when we meet the issue incompletely. So not only must we be aware of the nature and structure of the problem and see it completely, but meet it as it arises and resolve it immediately so that it does not take root in the mind. If one allows a problem to endure for a month or a day, or even for a few minutes, it distorts the mind. So is it possible to meet a problem immediately without any distortion and be immediately, completely, free of it and not allow a memory, a scratch on the mind, to remain? These memories are the images we carry about with us and it is these images that meet this extraordinary thing called life and therefore there is a contradiction and hence conflict. Life is very real—life is not an abstraction—and when you meet it with images there are problems.

Is it possible to meet every issue without this space-time interval, without the gap between oneself and the thing of which one is afraid? It is possible only when the observer has no continuity, the observer who is the builder of the image, the observer who is a collection of memories and ideas, who is a bundle of abstractions.

When you look at the stars, there is you who are looking at the stars in the sky; the sky is flooded with brilliant stars, there is cool air, and there is you, the observer, the experiencer, the thinker, you with your aching heart, you, the centre, creating space. You will never understand about the space between yourself and the stars, yourself and your wife or husband or friend, because you have never looked without the image, and that is why you do not know what beauty is or what love is. You talk about it, you write about it, but you have never known it except perhaps at rare intervals of total self-abandonment. So long as there is a centre creating space around itself there is neither love nor beauty. When there is no centre and no circumference then there is love. And when you love you *are* beauty.

When you look at a face opposite, you are looking from a centre and the centre creates the space between person and person, and that is why our lives are so empty and callous. You cannot cultivate love or beauty, nor can you invent truth, but if you are all the time aware of what you are doing, you can cultivate awareness. And out of that awareness you will begin to see the nature of pleasure, desire, and sorrow and the utter loneliness and boredom of man, and then you will begin to come upon that thing called "the space."

When there is space between you and the object you are observing you will know there is no love, and without love, however hard you try to reform the world or bring about a new social order or however much you talk about improvements, you will only create agony. So it is up to you. There is no leader, there is no teacher, there is nobody to tell you what to do. You are alone in this mad brutal world.

From Letters to the Schools
Volume 2, *1 November 1983*

ONE IS QUITE sure that the educators are aware of what is actually happening in the world. People are divided racially, religiously, politically, economically, and this division is fragmentation. It is bringing about great chaos in the world: wars, every kind of deception politically, and so on. There is the spreading of violence, man against man. This is the actual state of confusion in the world, in the society in which we live, and this society is created by all human beings with their cultures, their linguistic divisions, their regional separation. All this is breeding not only confusion but hatred, a great deal of antagonism, and further linguistic differences. This is what is happening and the responsibility of the educator is really very great.

❖

WHAT IS THIS education doing actually? Is it really helping man or his children to become more concerned, more gentle, or generous; is it helping him not to go back to the old pattern, the old ugliness and naughtiness of this world? If he is really concerned, as he must be, then he has to help the student to find out his relationship to the world, not to the world of imagination or romantic sentimentality, but to the actual world in which all things are taking place. And also to the world of nature, to the desert, the jungle, or the few trees that surround him, and to the animals of the world. Animals fortunately are not nationalistic; they hunt only to survive. If the educator and the student lose their relationship to nature, to the trees, to the rolling sea, each will certainly lose his relationship with man.

What is nature? There is a great deal of talk and endeavour to protect nature, the animals, the birds, the whales and dolphins, to clean the polluted rivers, the lakes, the green fields, and so on. Nature is not put together by thought, as religion is, as belief is. Nature is the tiger, that extraordinary animal with its energy, its great sense of power. Nature is the solitary tree in the field, the meadows and the grove; it is that squirrel shyly hiding behind a bough. Nature is the ant and the bee and all the living things of the earth. Nature is the river, not a particular river, whether the Ganges, the Thames, or the Mississippi. Nature is all those mountains, snowclad, with the dark blue valleys and range of hills meeting the sea. . . . One must have a feeling for all this, not destroy it, not kill for one's pleasure.

❖

NATURE IS PART of our life. We grew out of the seed, the earth, and we are part of all that, but we are rapidly losing the sense that we are animals like the others. Can you have a feeling for that tree? Look at it, see the beauty of it, listen to the sound it makes; be sensitive to the little plant, to the little weed, to that creeper that is growing up the wall, to the light on the leaves and the many shadows. You must be aware of all this and have that sense of communion with nature around you. You may live in a town but you do have trees here and there. A flower in the next garden may be ill-kept, crowded with weeds, but look at it, feel that you are part of all that, part of all living things. If you hurt nature you are hurting yourself.

You know all this has been said before in different ways, but we don't seem to pay much attention. Is it that we are so caught up in our own network of problems, our own desires, our own urges of pleasure and pain, that we never look around, never watch the moon? Watch it. Watch with all your eyes and ears, your sense of smell. Watch. Look as though you are looking for the first time. If you can do that, you are seeing that tree, that bush, that blade of grass for the first time. Then you can see your teacher, your mother and father, your brother and sister for the first time. There is an extraordinary feeling about that: the wonder, the strangeness, the miracle of a fresh morning that has never been before, never will be. Be really in communion with nature, not verbally caught in the description of it, but be a part of it, be aware, feel that you belong to all that, be able to have love for all that, to admire a deer, the lizard on the wall, that broken branch lying on the ground. Look at the evening star or the new moon, without the word, without merely saying how beautiful it is and turning your back on it, attracted by something else, but watch that single star and new delicate moon as though for the first time. If there is such communion between you and nature then you can commune with man, with the boy sitting next to you, with your educator, or with your parents. We have lost all sense of relationship in which there is not only a verbal statement of affection and concern but also this sense of communion that is not verbal. It is a sense that we are all together, that we are all human beings, not divided, not broken up, not belonging to any particular group or race, or to some idealistic concepts, but that we are all human beings, we are all living on this extraordinary, beautiful earth.

❖

THE EDUCATOR SHOULD talk about all these things, not just verbally but he himself must feel it—the world, the world of nature and the world of man. They are interrelated. Man cannot escape from that. When he destroys nature he is destroying himself. When he kills another he is killing himself. The enemy is not the other but you. To live in such harmony with nature, with the world, naturally brings about a different world.

From Letters to the Schools
Volume 2, *15 November 1983*

YOU LEARN A great deal by watching—watching the things about you, watching the birds, the trees, watching the heavens, the stars, the constellation of Orion, the Dipper, the evening star. You learn just by watching not only the things around you but also by watching people: how they walk, how they gesture, what words they use, how they dress. You not only watch that which is outside but also you watch yourself, why you think this or that, how you behave, how you conduct your daily life, why parents want you to do this or that. You are watching, not resisting. If you resist you don't learn. Or if you come to some kind of conclusion, some opinion you think is right, and hold on to that, then naturally you will never learn. Freedom is necessary to learn, and curiosity, a sense of wanting to know why you or others behave in a certain way, why people are angry, why you get annoyed.

❖

YOUR PARENTS, especially in the East, tell you whom you should marry and arrange the marriage; they tell you what your career should be. So the brain accepts the easy way and the easy way is not always the right way. I wonder if you have noticed that nobody loves their work any more, except perhaps a few scientists, artists, archaeologists. But the ordinary, average man seldom loves what he is doing. He is compelled by society, by his parents, or by the urge to have more money. So learn by watching very, very carefully the external world, the world outside you, and the inner world—that is, the world of yourself.

From Talks in Europe 1968, *Paris, 25 April 1968*

RELATIONSHIP CAN ONLY exist when there is total abandonment of the self, the "me." When the me is not, then you are related, in that there is no separation whatsoever. Probably one has not felt that, the total denial (not intellectually but actually), the total cessation of the me. And perhaps that's what most of us are seeking, sexually or through identification with something greater. But that again, that process of identification with something greater, is the product of thought; and thought is old (like the me, the ego, the I, it is of yesterday), it is always old. The question then arises: how is it possible to let go this isolating process completely, this process that is centred in the me. How is this to be done? You understand the question? How am I (whose every activity of everyday life is of fear, anxiety, despair, sorrow, confusion, and hope), how is the me that separates itself from another, through identification with god, with its conditioning, with its society, with its social and moral activity, with the State, and so on—how is that to die, to disappear so that the human being can be related? Because if we are not related, then we are going to live at war with each other. There may be no killing of each other because that is becoming too dangerous, except in faraway countries. How can we live so that there is no separation, so that we really can co-operate?

There is so much to do in the world: to wipe away poverty; to live happily; to live with delight instead of with agony and fear; to build a totally different kind of society, a morality that is above all morality. But this can only be when all the morality of present day society is totally denied. There is so much to do and it cannot be done if there is this constant isolating process going on. We speak of the "me" and the "mine" and the "other"—the other is beyond the wall, the me and mine is this side of the wall. So how can that essence of resistance, which is the me, how can that be completely "let go"? Because that is really the most fundamental question in all relationship, as one sees that the relationship between images is not relationship at all and that when that kind of relationship exists there must be conflict, that we must be at each other's throats.

When you put to yourself that question, inevitably you'll say, "Must I live in a vacuum, in a state of emptiness?" I wonder if you have ever known what it is to have a mind that is completely empty. You have lived in space that is created by the "me" (which is a very small space). The space that the "I," the self-isolating process, has built between one person and another is all the space we know—the space between itself and the circumference—the frontier that thought has built. And in this space we live, in this space there is division. You say, "If I let myself go, or if I abandon the centre of me, I will live in a vacuum." But have you ever really let go the me, actually, so that there is no me at all? Have you ever lived in this world, gone to the office in that spirit, lived with your wife or with your husband? If you have lived that way you will know that there is a state of relationship in which the me is not, which is not Utopia, which is not a thing dreamt about, or a mystical, nonsensical experience, but something that can be actually done—to live at a dimension where there is relationship with all human beings.

But that can only be when we understand what love is. And to be, to live in that state, one must understand the pleasure of thought and all its mechanism. Then all complicated mechanism that one has built for oneself, around oneself, can be seen at a glance. One hasn't got to go through all this analytical process point by point. All analysis is fragmentary, and therefore there is no answer through that door.

There is this immense complex problem of existence with all its fears, anxieties, hopes, fleeting happiness, and joys, but analysis is not going to solve it. What will do so is to take it all in swiftly, as a whole. You know you understand something only when you look—not with a prolonged trained look, the trained look of an artist, a scientist, or the man who has practised "how to look." You see it if you look at it with complete attention; you see the whole thing in one glance. And then you will see you are out of it. Then you are out of time; time has a stop and sorrow therefore ends. A man that is in sorrow, or fear, is not related. How can a man who is pursuing power have relationship? He may have a family, sleep with his wife, but he is not related. A man who is competing with another has no relationship at all. And all our social structure with its un-morality is based on this. To be fundamentally, essentially, related means the ending of the me that breeds separation and sorrow.

From Talks in Europe 1968, *Amsterdam, 22 May 1968*

As one observes what is happening in the world, the chaos, the confusion and the brutality of man to man, which no religion or social order—or perhaps disorder—has been able to prevent, as one observes the activities of the politicians, the economists, the social reformers, right throughout the world, one sees they have brought more and more confusion, more and more misery. Religions, that is organized beliefs, have certainly in no way helped to bring order, deep, abiding happiness to man. Nor have any Utopias, whether the Communist or those minority groups who have formed communities, brought any deep, lasting clarity to man. And one needs a tremendous revolution right throughout the world; a great change is necessary. We do not mean an outward revolution, but an inward revolution at the psychological level, which obviously is the only hope, is the only—if one can use the word—salvation for man. Ideologies have brought brutality, they have brought various forms of killing, wars; ideologies, however noble, are really quite ignoble. There must be a total mutation in the very structure of our brain cells, in the very structure of thought. And to bring about such deep lasting mutation, revolution, or change, one needs a great deal of energy. One needs a drive, a sustained, constant intensity, not the casual interest or passing enthusiasm that brings about a certain quality of energy, which is soon dissipated.... And that energy man has hoped to come by through resistance, through constant discipline, imitation, conformity.... Yet that resistance, conformity, discipline, mere adjustment to an idea, has not given man that necessary energy and force. So one has to find a different action that will bring this necessary energy.

In this present structure of society, in our relationship between man and man, the more we act, the less energy we have. For in that action there is contradiction, fragmentation, and so that action brings conflict and therefore wastes energy. One has to find the energy, which is sustaining, which is constant, which does not fade away. And I think there is such an action that brings about this vital quality that is necessary for a deep radical revolution in the mind. For most of us, action—that is "to do," to be active—takes place according to an idea, a formula, or a concept. If you observe your own activities, your own daily movement in action, you will see that you have formulated an idea or an ideology and according to that you act. So there is a division between the idea of what you should do, or what you should be, or how you should act, and actual action; you can see that in yourselves very clearly. So action is always approximation to the formula, to the concept, to the ideal. And there is a division, a separation, between what should be and what is, which causes duality and therefore there is conflict.

Please, do not merely listen to a series of words—words have no meaning in themselves, words have never brought about any radical change in man; you can pile up words, make a garland of them, as most of us do, and live on words, but they are ashes, they do not bring beauty into life. Words do not bring love, and if you are merely listening to a series of ideas or words, then I am afraid you will go empty-handed. But if you would listen, not only to the speaker, but to your own thoughts, listen to the way of your life, listen to what is being said not as something outside of you, but that is actually taking place within you, then you would see the reality—or the falseness—of what is being said. One has to see what is true and what is false for oneself, not through somebody else. And to find that out you have to listen, you have to give care, affection, attention, which means to be very serious, and life demands that we be serious, because it is only for the mind that is very serious that there is life—there is an abundance of life. But there is not to the curious, not to the intellectual, not to the emotionalist, not to the sentimentalist.

❖

WE NEED TREMENDOUS energy to bring about a psychological change in ourselves as human beings because we have lived far too long in a world of make-believe, in a world of brutality, violence, despair, anxiety. To live humanly, sanely, one has to change. To bring about a change within oneself and therefore within society, one needs this radical energy, for the individual is not different from society—the society is the individual and the individual is the society. And to bring about a necessary radical, essential change in the structure of society—which is corrupt, which is immoral—there must be change in the human heart and mind. To bring about that change you need great energy and that energy is denied or perverted or twisted when you act according to a concept, which is what we do in our daily life. The concept is based on past history, or on some conclusion, so it is not action at all, it is an approximation to a formula.

So one asks if there is an action that is not based on an idea, on a conclusion formed by dead things that have been.

❖

THERE IS SUCH action. Stating this is not the creation of another idea. One has to find out that action for oneself, and to find out, one has to begin right at the beginning of our human behaviour, of our human quality of mind. That is, we are never alone, we may be walking in a wood by ourselves, but we are not alone. You may be with your family, in society, but the human mind is so conditioned by past experience, knowledge, memory, that it does not know what it is to be alone. And one is afraid to be alone because to be alone implies—does it not?—that one has to be outside society. One may live in society, but one has to be an outsider to society. And to be an outsider to society one has to be free of society. Society demands that you act according to an idea; that is all society knows; that is all that human beings know—conform, imitate, accept, obey. And when one accepts the edicts of tradition, conforms to the pattern that society has set up (which means human beings have set up) then one is part of this whole conditioned human existence that wastes its energy through constant effort, constant conflict, confusion, misery. Is it possible for human beings to be free of this confusion, of this conflict?

Essentially this conflict is between the action and what that action should be. And one observes within oneself, as one must, how conflict constantly drains energy. The whole social structure—which is to be competitive, aggressive, comparing oneself with another, accepting an ideology, a belief, and so on—is based on conflict, not only within oneself but also outwardly. And we say, "If there is no conflict within oneself, no struggle, battle, we shall become like animals, we shall become lazy," which is not the actual fact. We do not know any other kind of life than the life we live, which is the constant struggle from the moment we are born until we die; that is all we know.

As one observes it one can see what a waste of energy it is. And one must extricate oneself from this social disorder, from this social immorality—which means one must be alone. Though you may live in society you are no longer accepting its structure and values—the brutality, the envy, the jealousy, the competitive spirit—and therefore you are alone, and when you are alone you are mature. Maturity is not of age.

Throughout the world there is revolt, but that revolt is not through the understanding of the whole structure of society, which is yourself. That revolt is fragmentary; that is, one may revolt against a particular war, or fight and kill another in one's favourite war, or be a religious believer belonging to a particular culture or group—Catholic, Protestant, Hindu, what you will. But to revolt means to revolt against the whole structure, not against a particular fragment of that culture. To understand this whole structure one must first be aware of it, one must first look at it, become conscious of it—that is, be choicelessly aware of it. You can't choose a particular part of society and say, "I like this, I don't like that, this pleases me and that does not please me." Then you are merely conforming to a particular pattern and resisting the other pattern, therefore you are still caught in the struggle. So what is important is first to see the picture of this whole human existence, the daily existence of our life. To see it—not as an idea, not as a concept, but actually be aware of it as one is aware of being hungry. Hunger is not an idea, it is not a concept, it is a fact. In the same way, to see this confusion, this misery, the constant endless struggle, when one is choicelessly aware of this whole thing, then there is no conflict at all; then one is outside the social structure because the mind has extricated itself from the absurdity of society.

❖

YOU KNOW, MAN—that is each one of us wherever we live—wants to find a state of mind, a state of living, which is not a travail, which is not a battle. I am sure all of us, however lowly or however intellectual we are, want to find a way of life that is orderly, full of beauty and great love. That has been the search of man for thousands of years. And instead of finding it he has externalized it, put it out there, created gods, saviours, priests with their ideas, and so he has missed the whole issue. One must deny all that, deny totally the acceptance that there is heaven through another, or by following another. Nobody in the world or in heaven can give you that life. One has to work for it—endlessly.

❖

I WONDER WHAT we mean by attitude. Why do we want an attitude? What does attitude mean? Taking up a position, coming to a conclusion. I have an attitude about whatever it is, which means I have come to a conclusion after study, after examining, after planning, after probing into the question. I have come to this point, to this attitude, which means that very assumption of an attitude is resistance; therefore that in itself is violence. We cannot have an attitude toward violence or hostility. That means you are interpreting it according to your particular conclusion, fancy, imagination, understanding. What we are asking is: Is it possible to look at this hostility in oneself, this creating enmity in oneself, this violence, this brutality in oneself, without any attitude, to see the fact as it is? The moment you have an attitude you are already prejudiced, you have taken a side, and therefore you are not looking, you are not understanding that fact within yourself.

❖

TO LOOK AT oneself without an attitude, without any opinion, judgment, evaluation, is one of the most arduous tasks. In this looking there is clarity, and it is that clarity that is not a conclusion, not an attitude, that dispels this total structure of brutality and hostility.

From Krishnamurti to Himself, *26 April 1983*

ONE SAW A BIRD dying, shot by a man. It was flying beautifully and with rhythmic beat, with such freedom and lack of fear. And the gun shattered it; it fell to the earth and all the life had gone out of it. A dog fetched it, and the man collected other dead birds. He was chattering with his friend and seemed so utterly indifferent. All that he was concerned with was bringing down so many birds, and it was over as far as he was concerned. They are killing all over the world. Those marvellous, great animals of the sea, the whales, are killed by the million, and the tiger and so many other animals are now becoming endangered species. Man is the only animal that is to be dreaded.

Some time ago, when staying with a friend high in the hills, a man came and told the host that a tiger had killed a cow the night before and asked if we would like to see the tiger that evening. He could arrange it by building a platform in a tree and tying up a goat. The bleat of the goat, of the small animal, would attract the tiger and we could see it. We both refused to satisfy our curiosity so cruelly. But later that day the host suggested that we get the car and go into the forest to see the tiger if we could. So toward evening we got into an open car with a chauffeur driving us and went deep into the forest for several miles. Of course we saw nothing. It was getting quite dark and the headlights were on, and as we turned around, there it was sitting right in the middle of the road waiting to receive us. It was a very large animal, beautifully marked, and its eyes, caught by the headlights, were bright, scintillating. It came growling toward the car, and as it passed just a few inches from the hand that was stretched out, the host said, "Don't touch it, it is too dangerous; be quick for it is faster than your hand." But you could feel the energy of that animal, its vitality; it was a great dynamo of energy. And as it passed by one felt an enormous attraction toward it. And it disappeared into the woods. [Krishnamurti tells of this meeting with a tiger more fully in his *Journal*, p. 40.]

Apparently the friend had seen many tigers and had helped long ago, in his youth, to kill one, and ever since he had been regretting the terrible act. Cruelty in every form is now spreading in the world. Man has probably never been so cruel as he is now, so violent. The churches and the priests of the world have talked about peace on earth; from the highest Christian hierarchy to the poor village priest there has been talk about living a good life, not hurting, not killing a thing. Especially the Buddhists and Hindus of former years have said, "Don't kill the fly, don't kill anything, for next life you will pay for it." That was rather crudely put, but some of them maintained this spirit, this intention not to kill and not to hurt another human being. But killing with wars is going on and on. The dog so quickly kills the rabbit. Or the man shoots another with his marvellous machines, and he himself is perhaps shot by another. And this killing has been going on for millennia upon millennia. Some treat it as a sport, others kill out of hatred, anger, jealousy; organized murder by the various nations with their armaments goes on. One wonders if man will ever live on this beautiful earth peacefully, never killing a living thing, or being killed, or killing another, but live peacefully with some divinity and love in his heart.

In this part of the world, which we call the West, the Christians have perhaps killed more than anyone else. They are always talking about peace on this earth. But to have peace one must live peacefully, and that seems so utterly impossible. There are arguments for and against war, arguments that man has always been a killer and will always remain so, and those who maintain that he can bring about a change in himself and not kill. This is a very old story. The endless butchering has become a habit, an accepted formula, in spite of all the religions.

One was watching the other day a red-tailed hawk, high in the heavens, circling effortlessly, without a beat of the wing, just for the fun of flying, just to be sustained by the air currents. Then it was joined by another, and they were flying together for quite a while. They were marvellous creatures in that blue sky, and to hurt them in any way is a crime against heaven. Of course there is no heaven; man has invented heaven out of hope, for his life has become a hell, an endless conflict from birth to death, coming and going, making money, working endlessly. This life has become a turmoil, a travail of endless striving. One wonders if man, a human being, will ever live on this earth peacefully. Conflict has been the way of his life—within the skin and outside the skin, in the area of the psyche and in the society which that psyche has created.

Probably love has totally disappeared from this world. Love implies generosity and care, not to hurt another, not to make another feel guilty, but to be generous, courteous, and behave in such a manner that your words and thoughts are born out of compassion. Of course you cannot be compassionate if you belong to organized religious institutions—large, powerful, traditional, dogmatic—that insist on faith. There must be freedom to love. That love is not pleasure, desire, a remembrance of things that have gone. Love is not the opposite of jealousy, hate, and anger.

All this may sound rather Utopian, idealistic, something that man can only aspire to. But if you believe that then you will go on killing. Love is as real, as strong, as death. It has nothing to do with imagination, or sentiment, or romanticism, and naturally it has nothing to do with power, position, prestige. It is as still as the waters of the sea and as powerful as the sea; it is like the running waters of a rich river flowing endlessly, without a beginning or an end. But the man who kills the baby seals, or the great whales, is concerned with his livelihood. He would say, "I live by that, that is my trade." He is totally unconcerned with that something that we call love. He probably loves his family—or he thinks he loves his family—and he is not very much concerned with how he gains his livelihood. Perhaps that is one of the reasons why man lives a fragmentary life; he never seems to love what he is doing—though perhaps a few people do. If one lived by the work one loves, it would be very different—one would understand the wholeness of life. We have broken up life into fragments: the business world, the artistic world, the scientific world, the political world, and the religious world. We seem to think that they are all separate and should be kept separate. So we become hypocritical, doing something ugly, corrupt, in the business world and then coming home to live peacefully with our family; this breeds hypocrisy, a double standard of life.

It is really a marvellous earth. That bird sitting on the tallest tree has been sitting there every morning, looking over the world, watching for a greater bird, a bird that might kill it, watching the clouds, the passing shadow, and the great spread of this rich earth, these rivers, forests, and all the men who work from morning until night. If one thinks at all, in the psychological world, it is to be full of sorrow. One wonders too if man will ever change, or only the few, the very, very few. Then what is the relationship of the few to the many? Or, what is the relationship of the many to the few? The many have no relationship to the few. The few do have a relationship.

Sitting on that rock, looking down into the valley, with a lizard beside you, you daren't move in case the lizard should be disturbed or frightened. And the lizard too is watching. And so the world goes on: inventing gods, following the hierarchy of the gods' representatives. And all the sham and the shame of illusions will probably go on, the thousand problems getting more and more complex and intricate. Only the intelligence of love and compassion can solve all problems of life. That intelligence is the only instrument that can never become dull, useless.

Brockwood Park,
10 September 1970

We REALIZE THERE is a division in life, in me, in you. The you and me are many fragments. Oneself is made up of many fragments. One of the fragments is the observer and the rest of the fragments are the observed. The observer becomes conscious of the fragments, but the observer is also one of the fragments; he is not different from the rest of the fragments. Therefore you have to find out what is the observer, the experiencer, the thinker. What is he made up of, how does it come about, this division between the observer and the observed? The observer, we say, is one of the fragments. Why has he separated himself, assumed himself as the analyzer, the one who is aware, the one who can control, change, suppress, and all the rest of it. The observer is the censor . . . the result of the social, environmental, religious, cultural conditionings. That is, the cultural divisions have said you are different from the thing you are observing. . . . You are the higher self and that is the lower self, you are the enlightened and that is unenlightened. Now what has given him this authority to call himself enlightened? Because he has become the censor? And the censor says, "This is right, this is wrong, this is good, this is bad, I must do this, I must not do that," which is the result of his conditioning, the conditioning of the society, of the culture, of the religion, of the family, of all the race, and so on.

So the observer is the censor, conditioned according to his environment. And he has assumed the authority of the analyzer. And the rest of the fragments are also assuming their authority; each fragment has its own authority, and so there is battle. And so there is conflict between the observer and the observed. To be free of this conflict you have to find out if you can look without the eyes of the censor. That is to be aware, to be aware that the eyes of the censor are the result of his conditioning. And can those eyes look with freedom, look innocently, freely?

❖

CAN THE MIND be free of all this conditioning? . . . I am conditioned by a culture that has existed for thousands of years. . . . Can the brain cells themselves be free of all conditioning as the observer, as an entity that is conforming, as an entity that is conditioned by the environment, culture, family, race? If the mind is not free from conditioning it can never be free of conflict and therefore neuroticism. . . . Unless we are completely free, we are unbalanced people. And out of our unbalance we do all kinds of mischief.

So maturity is freedom from conditioning. And that freedom is obviously not the result of the observer, which is the very source of all memory, of all thought. Can I look with eyes that have never been touched by the past? And that is sanity. Can you look at the cloud, the tree, your wife, your husband, your friend, without an image? To be aware that you have an image is the first thing, isn't it? To be aware that you are looking at life through a formula, through an image, through concepts, which are all distorting factors. And to be aware of it without any choice. And as long as the observer is aware of these then there is distortion. Therefore, can you look, can the mind observe without the censor? Can you listen without any interpretation, without any comparison, judgment, evaluation, listen to that breeze, to that wind, without any interference of the past?

Saanen, 13 July 1975

THOUGHT IS THE response of memory as experience and knowledge, so we are always operating in the field of knowledge. And knowledge has not changed man. We have had thousands of wars, millions of human beings have suffered, cried, and we still carry on! The knowledge of war has not taught us anything, except how to kill better, on a vaster scale. Knowledge has not changed man; we accept division, nationalities. We accept that division though it will inevitably bring about conflict with each other; we have accepted the injustice, the cruelty that thought has brought about through knowledge. We are destroying species of animals: fifty million whales have been killed from the beginning of this century. Everything man touches brings about destruction. So thought which is the response of memory, experience, knowledge, has not changed man, though it has created an extraordinary technological world.

❖

WHEN THE MIND realizes the limitation, the narrowness, the finiteness of thought, then only can it ask the question: What is truth? Is this clear? I do not accept truth given by philosophers—that's their game. Philosophy means love of truth, not love of thought. So there is no authority—Plato, Socrates, Buddha. And Christianity has not gone into this very deeply. It has played with words and symbols, made a parody of suffering and all the rest of it. So the mind rejects all that.

❖

THEN, WHAT IS truth? . . . You have got to sweat your blood to do this thing, got to give your heart to this, not just accept some silly thing. You have to have the capacity to investigate, not the capacity that time cultivates, like learning a technique, but this capacity comes when you are really, deeply concerned, when it is a matter of life and death—you understand?—to find out.

From Krishnamurti to Himself, *25 February 1983*

THERE IS A TREE by the river and we have been watching it day after day for several weeks when the sun is about to rise. As the sun rises slowly over the horizon, over the trees, this particular tree becomes all of a sudden golden. All the leaves are bright with life, and as you watch them as the hours pass by, that tree whose name does not matter—what matters is that beautiful tree—the watching seems to spread an extraordinary quality all over the land, over the river. And as the sun rises a little higher the leaves begin to flutter, to dance. And each hour seems to give to that tree a different quality. Before the sun rises it has a sombre feeling, quiet, far away, full of dignity. And as the day begins, the leaves with the light on them dance and give it that peculiar feeling that one has of great beauty. By midday its shadow has deepened and you can sit there protected from the sun, never feeling lonely, with the tree as your companion. As you sit there, there is a relationship of deep abiding security and a freedom that only trees can know.

Toward the evening when the western skies are lit up by the setting sun, the tree gradually becomes sombre, dark, closing in on itself. The sky has become red, yellow, green, but the tree remains quiet, hidden, and is resting for the night.

If you establish a relationship with it, then you have relationship with mankind. You are responsible then for that tree and for the trees of the world. But if you have no relationship with the living things on this earth, you may lose whatever relationship you have with humanity, with human beings. We never look deeply into the quality of a tree; we never really touch it, feel its solidity, its rough bark, and hear the sound that is part of the tree. Not the sound of wind through the leaves, not the breeze of a morning that flutters the leaves, but its own sound, the sound of the trunk and the silent sound of the roots. You must be extraordinarily sensitive to hear the sound. This sound is not the noise of the world, not the noise of the chattering of the mind, not the vulgarity of human quarrels and human warfare, but sound as part of the universe.

It is odd that we have so little relationship with nature, with the insects and the leaping frog and the owl that hoots among the hills calling for its mate. We never seem to have a feeling for all living things on the earth. If we could establish a deep abiding relationship with nature, we would never kill an animal for our appetite, we would never harm, vivisect, a monkey, a dog, a guinea pig for our benefit. We would find other ways to heal our wounds, heal our bodies. But the healing of the mind is something totally different. That healing gradually takes place if you are with nature, with that orange on the tree, and the blade of grass that pushes through the cement, and the hills covered, hidden, by the clouds.

This is not sentiment or romantic imagination but a reality of a relationship with everything that lives and moves on the earth. Man has killed millions of whales and is still killing them. All that we derive from their slaughter can be had through other means. But apparently man loves to kill things, the fleeting deer, the marvellous gazelle, and the great elephant. We love to kill each other. This killing of other human beings has never stopped throughout the history of man's life on this earth. If we could, and we must, establish a deep long abiding relationship with nature, with the actual trees, the bushes, the flowers, the grass, and the fast moving clouds, then we would never slaughter another human being for any reason whatsoever. Organized murder is war.

Brockwood Park,
4 September 1980

Questioner: Why is it that in the balance of nature there is always death and suffering?

Krishnamurti: Why is it man has killed fifty million whales? Fifty million—you understand? And still we are killing every kind of species—the tigers are coming to an end, the cheetahs, the leopards and elephants, for their flesh, for their tusks—you know all that. Is not man a much more dangerous animal than the rest of the animals? And you want to know why in nature there is death and suffering. You see a tiger killing a cow, or a deer. That is their natural way of life, but the moment we interfere with it, it becomes real cruelty. You have seen baby seals being knocked on the head, and, when there is a great protest against it, the Unions say that we have to live that way. You know all this.

So where shall we start to understand the world about us and the world within us? The world within us is so enormously complex that we want to understand the world of nature first. ... Perhaps if we could start with ourselves, not to hurt, not to be violent, not to be nationalistic, but to feel for the whole of mankind, then perhaps we shall have a proper relationship between ourselves and nature. Now we are destroying the earth, the air, the sea, the things of the sea, because we are the greatest danger to the world, with our atomic bombs—you know, all that kind of thing.

Q: You say we are the world, but the majority of the world seems to be heading for mass destruction. Can a minority of integrated people outweigh the majority?

K: Are you the minority? No, I am not joking. It is not a callous question. Are we the minority? Or is there one among us who is totally free of all this? Or are we partially contributing to the hatred of each other? Psychologically. You may not be able to stop Russia or America, England or Japan from attacking some other country, but psychologically are we free of our common inheritance, which is our tribal, glorified nationalism? Are we free from violence? Violence exists where there is a wall around ourselves. Please understand all this. And we have built ourselves walls, ten feet high or fifteen feet thick. All of us have walls around us. And from that arises violence, this sense of immense loneliness. So the minority and the majority is you. If a group of us fundamentally have psychologically transformed ourselves you will never ask this question, because we are then something entirely different.

Q: If there is a supreme truth and order why does it allow mankind to behave on earth in such a shocking way?

K: If there is such a supreme entity, he must be very odd, because if he created us then we are part of him—right? And if he is ordered, sane, rational, compassionate, we wouldn't be like this. You can accept the evolutionary process of man, or believe that man has suddenly come into being created by god. And god, that supreme entity, is order, goodness, compassion, and all the rest of it, all the attributes that we give to it. So you have these two choices, that there is a supreme entity who made man according to his image, or that there is the evolutionary process of man, which life has brought about from the beginning of small molecules and so on, right up to now.

If you accept the idea of god, the supreme person in whom total order exists, and you are part of that entity, then that person must be extraordinarily cruel—right?—extraordinarily intolerant to make us behave as we are doing, destroying each other.

Or, there is the other, which is that man has made the world as it is; human beings have made this world, the social world, the world of relationship, the technological world, the world of society—our relationship with each other. We, not god or some supreme entity, have made it. We are responsible for this horror that we have perpetuated. And to rely on a certain external agency to transform all this, that game has been played for millennia and you are still the same! Perhaps a little changed, a little more kind, a little more tolerant—but tolerance is something ugly.

Questioner: You have talked of standing up against the corrupt and immoral society. Further clarification is very important to me.

Krishnamurti: First of all, are we clear what the word *corruption* implies? There is the physical corruption of the pollution of the air, in cities, in manufacturing towns. We are destroying the seas, we are killing millions of whales and baby seals. There is physical pollution in the world, and there is overpopulation. Then there is the corruption politically, religiously, and so on. At what depth is this corruption in the human brain, in the human activity? We must be very clear when we talk about corruption what we mean by that word, and at what level we are talking about it.

Throughout the world there is corruption. And more so, unfortunately, in this part of the world—passing money under the table, having to bribe if you want to buy a ticket—you know all the games that go on in this country. The word *corrupt* means to break up, not only various parts against other communities and states, but basically corruption of the brain and the heart. So we must be clear at what level we are talking about this corruption: at the financial level, at the bureaucratic level, the political level, or the religious level—which is ridden with all kinds of superstition, without any sense at all, just a lot of words that have lost all meaning, both in the Christian world and in the Eastern world. The repetition of rituals, you know all that goes on. Is that not corruption? Please, let's talk it over.

Are not ideals a form of corruption? We may have ideals. Say, for example, non-violence. When you have ideals of non-violence that you pursue, in the meantime you are violent. Right? So is that not corruption of a brain that disregards the action to end violence? That seems very clear.

And is there not corruption when there is no love at all, only pleasure, with its suffering? Throughout the world this word is heavily loaded, and, being associated with sex, pleasure, anxiety, jealousy, and attachment, is that not corruption? Is not attachment itself corruption? When one is attached to an ideal, to a house, or to a person, the consequences are jealousy, anxiety, possessiveness, domination.

So the question is basically about the society in which we live that is essentially based on relationship with each other. If there is no love, just mutual exploitation, mutual comforting each other sexually, and in various other ways, that relationship must inevitably bring about corruption. So what will you do about all this? That's really the question: What will you do, as a human being, living in this world, which is a marvellous world? The beauty of the earth, the sense of the extraordinary quality of a tree—we are destroying the earth, as we are destroying ourselves! So what will you, as a human being living here, do? Will we, each one of us, see that we are not corrupt? We create the abstraction that we call society. If our relationship with each other is destructive—constant battle, struggle, pain, despair—then we will inevitably create an environment that will represent what we are. So what are we going to do about it, each one of us? Is this corruption, this sense of lack of integrity, an abstraction? Is it an idea or an actuality that we want to change? It's up to you.

Q: Is there really such a thing as transformation? What is it to be transformed?

K: When you are observing, seeing around you, the dirt on the road, your politicians and how they behave, your own attitude toward your wife, your children, and so on, transformation is there. You understand? To bring about some kind of order in daily life, that is transformation, not something extraordinary, outside the world. That is, when one is not thinking clearly, objectively, sanely, rationally, one must be aware of that and change it, break it. That is transformation. If I am jealous, I must watch it, and not give it time to flower. Change it immediately. That is transformation. When you are greedy, violent, ambitious—whether trying to become some kind of god or holy man, or in business—see the whole business of ambition, how it is creating a world of tremendous ruthlessness. I don't know if you are aware of all this. Competition is destroying the world, which is becoming more and more aggressive. If you are aware, change it immediately. That is transformation.

❖

Q: You say that if one individual changes he can transform the world. Yet in spite of your sincerity, love, clarity, and that power which cannot be described, the world has gone from bad to worse. Is there such a thing as destiny?

K: What is the world? What is the individual? What have individuals done that has influenced the world? Hitler has influenced the world. Right? Mao Tse-tung, Stalin, Lenin, and Lincoln have influenced it, and also, totally differently, the Buddha. One person killed millions and millions of people. All the warmongers, the generals, have killed, killed, killed. That has affected the world. Within the last historical five thousand years, since history has been kept, there has been a war every year, affecting millions of people. And then you have the Buddha: he has also affected the human mind, the human brain, throughout the East. And there have been those who have distorted. So when we ask if individual change brings about any transformation in society, I think that is a wrong question to put.

Are we really concerned about the transformation of society? If you go into it seriously, are we really concerned? Society that is corrupt, that is immoral, that is based on competition and ruthlessness—that society in which we are living—are you deeply interested in changing that, even as a single human being? If you are, then you have to inquire what is society. Is society a word? Is it a reality, or is it an abstraction? You understand? An abstraction of human relationship. It is human relationship that is society. That relationship, with all its complexities, contradictions, and hatreds—can you alter all that? You can. You can stop being cruel, you know, all the rest of it. What your relationship is, your environment is. If your relationship is possessive, and self-centred, you are creating a thing around you that will be equally destructive. So the individual is you; you are the rest of mankind. I don't know if you realize it. Psychologically, inwardly, you suffer. You are anxious, you are lonely, you are competitive; you try to be something, and this is the common factor throughout the world. Every human being throughout the world is doing this, so you are actually the rest of mankind. If you perceive that, and if you bring about a different way of living in yourself, you are affecting the whole consciousness of mankind. That is if you are really serious and go into it deeply. If you don't, it's all right, it's up to you.

Saanen, 29 July 1981

Questioner: How can the idea of, "You are the world and you are totally responsible for the whole of mankind," be justified on a rational, objective, sane basis?

Krishnamurti: I am not sure that it can be rationalized on a sane, objective basis. But we will examine it first before we say it can't!

First of all the earth on which we live is our earth—right? It is not the British earth, the French earth, or the German, Russian, Indian, Chinese, it is our earth on which we are all living. That is a fact. But thought has divided it racially, geographically, culturally, economically. That division is causing havoc in the world—obviously. There is no denial of that. That statement is rational, objective, sane. It is our earth on which we are all living, but we have divided it—for security, for various patriotic, political, illusory reasons, which eventually bring about war.

We have also said that all human consciousness is similar. We all, on whatever part of the earth we live, go through a great deal of suffering, pain, anxiety, uncertainty, fear. And we have occasionally, or perhaps often, pleasure. This is the common ground on which all human beings stand—right? This is an irrefutable fact. We may try to dodge it, we may try to say it is not, that I am an individual and so on, but when you look at it objectively, non-personally, you will find that our consciousness is like the consciousness of all human beings, psychologically. You may be tall, you may be fair, you may have brown hair; I may be black, or white, or pink, or whatever—but inwardly we are all having a terrible time. We all have a sense of desperate loneliness. You may have children, a husband, family, but when you are alone you have this feeling that you have no relationship with anything. You feel totally isolated. Most of us have had that feeling. This is the common ground of all humanity. And whatever happens in the field of this consciousness, we are responsible. That is, if I am violent, I am adding violence to that consciousness that is common to all of us. If I am not violent, I am not adding to it; I am bringing a totally new factor to that consciousness. So I am profoundly responsible: either I contribute to that violence, to that confusion, to that terrible division, or, as I recognize deeply in my heart, in my blood, in the depths of my being, that I am the rest of the world, I am mankind, I am the world, the world is not separate from me, then I become totally responsible. Obviously! This is rational, objective, sane. The other is insanity—to call oneself a Hindu, a Buddhist, a Christian, and all the rest of it—these are just labels.

When one has that feeling, that reality, the truth that every human being living on this earth is responsible not only for himself, but for everything that is happening, how will one translate that in daily life? Do you have that feeling, not as an intellectual conclusion, an ideal, and so on? Then it has no reality. But if the truth is that you are standing on the ground that is common to all mankind, and you feel totally responsible, then what is your action toward society, toward the world in which you are actually living? The world as it is now is full of violence. Suppose I realize I am totally responsible. What is my action? Shall I join a group of terrorists? Obviously not. Clearly competitiveness between nations is destroying the world. When I feel responsible for this, naturally I cease to be competitive. And the religious world as well as the economic, social world is based on hierarchical principle. Shall I also have this concept of hierarchical outlook? Obviously not, because the one who says, "I know," is taking a superior position, and has a status. If you want that status, go after it, but you are contributing to the confusion of the world.

So there are actual, objective, sane actions when you perceive, when you realize in your heart of hearts, that you are the rest of mankind, and that we are all standing on the same ground.

From From Darkness to Light

The Song of Life

Love not the shapely branch,
Nor place its image alone in thy heart.
It dieth away.

Love the whole tree.
Then thou shalt love the shapely branch,
The tender and the withered leaf,
The shy bud and the full-blown flower,
The falling petal and the dancing height,
The splendid shadow of full love.

Ah, love Life in its fullness.
It knoweth no decay.

From Krishnamurti to Himself, *6 May 1983*

SITTING ON THE beach watching the people pass by, two or three couples and a single woman, it seems that all nature, everything around you, from the deep blue sea to those high rocky mountains, is also watching. We are watching, not waiting, nor expecting anything to happen but watching without end. In that watching there is learning, not the accumulation of knowledge through learning that is almost mechanical, but watching closely, never superficially but deeply, with a swiftness and a tenderness; then there is no watcher. When there is a watcher it is merely the past watching, and that is not watching, that is just remembering, and it is rather dead stuff. Watching is tremendously alive, every moment a vacancy. Those little crabs and those seagulls and all those birds flying by are watching. They are watching for prey, for fish, watching for something to eat; they too are watching. Somebody passes close by you and wonders what you are watching. You are watching nothing, and in that nothingness everything is.

The other day a man who had travelled a great deal, seen a great deal, written something or other, came—an oldish man with a beard, which was well kept. He was dressed decently without the sloppiness of vulgarity. He took care of his shoes, of his clothes. He spoke excellent English, though he was a foreigner. And to the man who was sitting on the beach watching, he said he had talked to a great many people, discussed with some professors and scholars, and while he was in India he had talked to some of the pundits. And most of them, it seemed, according to him, were not concerned with society, not deeply committed to any social reform or to the present crisis of war. He was deeply concerned about the society in which we were living, though he was not a social reformer. He was not quite sure whether society could be changed, whether you could do something about it. But he saw what it was: the vast corruption, the absurdity of the politicians, the pettiness, the vanity, and the brutality that is rampant in the world.

He said, "What can we do about this society?—not petty little reforms here and there, changing one president for another, or one prime minister for another—they are all of the same breed more or less; they can't do much because they represent the mediocrity, or even less than that, the vulgarity; they want to show off, they will never do anything. They will bring about potty little reforms here and there but society will go on in spite of them." He had watched the various societies, cultures. They are not so very different fundamentally. He appeared to be a very serious man with a smile, and he talked about the beauty of this country, the vastness, the variety, from the hot deserts to the high Rockies with their splendour. One listened to him as one would listen to and watch the sea.

Society cannot be changed unless man changes. Man, you and others, have created these societies for generations upon generations; we have all created these societies out of our pettiness, narrowness, out of our limitation, out of our greed, envy, brutality, violence, competition, and so on. We are responsible for the mediocrity, the stupidity, the vulgarity, for all the tribal nonsense and religious sectarianism. Unless each one of us changes radically, society will never change. It is there, we have made it, and then it makes us. It shapes us, as we have shaped it. It puts us in a mould and the mould puts it into a framework, which is the society.

So this action is going on endlessly, like the sea with a tide that goes far out and then comes in, sometimes very, very slowly, at other times rapidly, dangerously. In and out; action, reaction, action. This seems to be the nature of this movement, unless there is deep order in oneself. That very order will bring about order in society, not through legislation, governments and all that business—though as long as there is disorder, confusion, the law, the authority, which is created by our disorder, will go on. Law is the making of man, as the society is—the product of man is law.

So the inner, the psyche, creates the outer according to its limitation; and the outer then controls and moulds the inner. The Communists have thought, and probably still do, that by controlling the outer, bringing about certain laws, regulations, institutions, certain forms of tyranny, they can change man. But so far they have not succeeded, and they never will succeed. This is also the activity of the Socialists. The Capitalists do it in a different way, but it is the same thing. The inner always overcomes the outer, for the inner is far more strong, far more vital, than the outer.

Can this movement ever stop—the inner creating the outer environment psychologically, and the outer, the law, the institutions, the organizations, trying to shape man, the brain, to act in a certain way, and the brain, the inner, the psyche, then changing, circumventing the outer? This movement has been going on as long as man has been on this earth, crudely, superficially, sometimes brilliantly—it is always the inner overcoming the outer, like the sea with its tides going out and coming in. One should really ask whether this movement can ever stop—action and reaction, hatred and more hatred, violence and more violence. It has an end when there is only watching, without motive, without response, without direction.

Direction comes into being when there is accumulation. But watching, in which there is attention, awareness, and a great sense of compassion, has its own intelligence. This watching and intelligence act. And that action is not the ebb and flow. But this requires great alertness, to see things without the word, without the name, without any reaction; in that watching there is a great vitality, passion.

Madras, 27 December 1981

WE HAVE BEEN talking about conflict, and whether all the human beings who have lived on this earth, with all its vast treasures, have been in perpetual conflict. Not only outwardly with the environment, with nature, but with each other, and inwardly, so-called spiritually; we have been in constant conflict. From the moment we are born until we die we are in conflict. And we put up with it; we have become accustomed to it; we tolerate it. We find many reasons why we should live in conflict. We think struggle and constant striving mean progress, outward progress, or inward achievement toward the highest goal.

This beautiful country, India, is lovely hills, marvellous mountains, tremendous rivers. But after thousands of years of suffering, struggle, obeying, accepting, destroying each other, this is what we have reduced it to, a wilderness of wild thoughtless human beings, who do not care for the earth, nor for the lovely things of the earth, for the beauty of a lake, of the swift running river. None of us seems to care. All that we are concerned with is our own little selves, our own little problems. One wants to cry with what we are doing in this country, and with what other countries are doing.

Life has become extraordinarily dangerous, insecure, without any meaning. You may invent a lot of significance, but actual daily life has lost all meaning except to gather money, to be somebody, to be powerful and so on.

And no politician, whether of the left, right, or centre, is going to solve any of our problems. Politicians are not interested in solving problems. They are only concerned with themselves and keeping their position. And the gurus and religions have also betrayed man. You have followed the Upanishads, the Brahmasutras, and Bhagavad Gita, and it's the guru's game to read them aloud to an audience that is supposed to be enlightened, intelligent. So you cannot possibly rely on the politicians, that is government, nor upon the scriptures or any guru whatsoever, because they have made this country what it is now. If one seeks further leadership, that will also lead you up the wrong path. And as no one can help us, we have to be totally, completely responsible for our conduct, our behaviour, and our actions.

❖

THIS COUNTRY HAS always talked about non-violence. This has been preached over and over again, politically, religiously, by various leaders, but non-violence is not a fact, just an idea, a theory, a set of words. The actual fact is that you are violent. That's what is. And we are not capable of understanding "what is," and that is why we create this nonsense called non-violence. So that becomes a conflict between "what is" and "what should be." And while you are pursuing non-violence, you are sowing the seeds of violence all the time. That is again so obvious. So can we together look at "what is" without any escape, without any ideals, without suppressing or moving away from it? We are violent by inheritance from the animal, from the ape and so on. Violence takes many forms, not merely brutal action; it is a very complicated issue. Violence is imitation, conformity, obedience; violence is pretending you are what you are not; that is a form of violence. Please see the logic of all this. It is not just that we are making statements for you to accept or deny. We are walking down a path, in a forest, in the lovely woods, together and investigating violence, like two friends talking things over together, without any persuasion, without any sense of resolution of the problem. We are talking together, we are observing together. We are walking along the same path, not your path or my path, but the path of investigation into these problems.

❖

SO WE HAVE to learn together how to observe. You are not the speaker's followers, he is not your guru, thank god; there is no superior or inferior in this investigation. There is no authority. When your mind is crippled with authority, it is very difficult to look at violence. So it is important to understand how to observe what is happening in the world: the misery, the confusion, the hypocrisy, the lack of integrity, the brutal actions that are going on, the terrorists, the people who are taking hostages, and the gurus who have their own particular concentration camps! It is all violence. How can anyone say, "I know, follow me"? That is a scandalous statement. So we are together observing what violence is, and asking, what is it to observe? What is it to observe the environment around you: the trees, that pond in the corner, the stars, the new moon, the solitary Venus, the evening star, the glory of a sunset? How do you watch it? You cannot watch, observe, if you are occupied with yourself, your own problems, your ideas, your own complex thinking. Right? You cannot observe if you have prejudice, or if there is any kind of conclusion or particular experience to which you cling. So how do you observe this marvellous thing called a tree? How do you look at it now, as you are sitting there surrounded by these trees? Have you seen their leaves, fluttering in the wind, the beauty of the light on the leaf; have you ever watched it? So can you watch a tree, or the new moon, or the single star in the heavens without the word? Because the word is not the actual star, the actual moon. Can you put aside the word and look?

Can you look at your wife without the word? Without all the remembrance of your relationship, however intimate it has been, without all that built-up memory. Can you look at your wife, or your husband, without the memory of the past? Have you ever done it? Please let us learn together how to observe a flower. If you know how to look at a flower, that contains eternity. Don't be carried away by my words! If you know how to look at a star, a dense forest, then in that observation there is space, eternity. We must together find out how to observe your wife or your husband without the image you have created about her or him. You must begin very close in order to go very far. If you don't begin close you can never go far. If you want to climb the mountain or go to the next village, the first steps matter: how you walk, with what grace, with what ease, with what felicity. So we are saying that to go very, very far, which is eternity, you must begin very close, which is your relationship with your partner. Can you observe your family with clear eyes without the words "my wife," or "my husband," "my nephew," or "my son"? Without the word, without all the accumulated hurts and the remembrance of things past. Do it now. Observe. And when you are capable of observing without the past, that is all the images you have built about yourself and about them, then there is right relationship.

❖

WHEN YOU LIVE everyday with "what is" and observe "what is," not only out there but inwardly, then you will create a society that will be without conflict.

Bombay, 24 January 1982

WE ARE GOING to talk over together the relationship between a human being and nature, which is the relationship between yourself and the environment. The environment is not only the city or the town or the village you live in, but also the environment of nature. If you have no relationship with nature you have no relationship with man. Nature is the meadows, the groves, the rivers, all the marvellous earth, the trees, and the beauty of the earth. If we have no relationship with that, we shall have no relationship with each other. Because thought has not created nature, thought has not made the tiger or the waters of an evening with the stars on them. Thought hasn't created the vast snow-capped mountains against the blue sky, the sunset and the lonely moon when there is no other star. So thought has not created nature.

Nature is a reality. What we have created between human beings is also a reality, but a reality in which there is conflict, there is struggle, everyone is trying to become something. Both physically and inwardly, and, if I may use that word, spiritually. When one is trying to become, trying to achieve some status politically or religiously, then one has no relationship with another, nor with nature. Many of you live in cities with all the crowds, noise, and dirt in the environment. Probably you have not often come across nature. But there is this marvellous sea, and you have no relationship to it. You look at it, perhaps you swim there, but the feeling of this sea with its enormous vitality and energy, the beauty of a wave crashing upon the shore—there is no communication between that marvellous movement of the sea and yourself. And if you have no relationship with that, how can you have relationship with another human being? If you don't perceive the sea, the quality of the water, the waves, the great vitality of the tide going out and coming in, how can you be aware, or be sensitive to human relationship? Please, it is very important to understand this, because beauty, if one may talk about it, is not merely in the physical form, but beauty in essence is that quality of sensitivity, the quality of observation of nature.

Ojai, 1 May 1982

THE CRISIS IS NOT economic, war, the bomb, the politicians, the scientists, but the crisis is within us, the crisis is in our consciousness. Until we understand very profoundly the nature of that consciousness, and question, delve deeply into it and find out for ourselves whether there can be a total mutation in that consciousness, the world will go on creating more misery, more confusion, more horror. So our responsibility is not some kind of altruistic action, political, or economic, but to comprehend the nature of our being—why we human beings, who have lived on this beautiful lovely earth, have become like this.

So if you are willing, if it is your responsibility, we can perceive together the nature of our consciousness, the nature of our being. This is not a lecture, but we are trying, you and the speaker together, not separately, to observe the movement of this consciousness and its relationship to the world, whether that consciousness is individual, separate, or that consciousness is of the whole of mankind. We are educated from childhood to be individuals, with separate souls—if you believe in that kind of stuff. You have been trained, educated, conditioned to think as an individual. We think because we have separate names, separate forms—dark, light, tall, short, fair, black, and so on—and our particular tendencies and experiences, that we are separate individuals. Now we are going to question that very idea: are we individuals?

It doesn't mean that we are a kind of amorphous being, but actually are we individuals? The whole world maintains, both religiously and in other ways, that we are separate individuals. And from that concept, perhaps from that illusion, each one of us trying to fulfil, to become something, is competing against another, fighting another. So if we maintain that way of life, we must inevitably cling to nationalities, tribalism, war. Why do we hold on to nationalism and the passion behind it, which is what is happening now? Why do we give such extraordinary importance to nationalism, which is essentially tribalism? Why? Is it because in holding on to the tribe, to the group, there is certain security—not only physical security but psychological security, an inward sense of completeness, fullness? If that is so, then the other tribe also feels the same; hence division and hence war, conflict.

If one actually sees the truth of this, not theoretically, and if one wants to live on this earth, which is our earth, not yours or mine, American or Russian or Hindu, then there is no nationalism at all. There is only human existence. One life—it's not your life or my life, it's living the whole of life. But this tradition of individuality has been perpetuated by religions both in the East and in the West.

Now is this so? You know, it is very good to doubt, very good to have a mind that questions, doesn't accept; a mind that says, we cannot possibly live any more like this, in this brutal, violent manner. So doubt, questioning, has extraordinary importance; not just accepting the way of life we have lived perhaps for thirty years, or the way man has lived for a million years. So we are questioning the reality of individuality.

To be conscious means to be aware, to know, to perceive, to observe. The content of consciousness is your belief, your pleasure, your experience, the particular knowledge that you have gathered, either through external experience or through your fears, attachments, pain, the agony of loneliness, sorrow, the search for something more than mere physical existence; all that is one's consciousness with its content. The content makes the consciousness.

Without content there is not the consciousness as we know it. That consciousness, which is very complex, contradictory, with extraordinary vitality, is it yours? Is thought yours? Or is there only thinking, which is neither of the East nor the West? There is only thinking, which is common to all mankind, whether rich or poor. Technicians, with their extraordinary capacity, or the monks who withdraw from the world and consecrate themselves to an idea, are still thinking.

Is this consciousness common to all mankind? Wherever one goes, one sees suffering, pain, anxiety, loneliness, insanity, fear, the urge of desire. It is common, it is the ground on which every human being stands. Your consciousness is the consciousness of humanity, the rest of humanity. If one understands the nature of this—that you are the rest of mankind, though we may have different names, live in different parts of the world, be educated in different ways, be affluent or very poor—when you go behind the mask, you are like the rest of mankind: neurotic, aching, suffering loneliness and despair, believing in some illusion, and so on. Whether you go to the East or West, this is so. You may not like it; you may like to think that you are totally independent, free, individual. But when you observe very deeply, you are the rest of humanity.

Madras, 26 December 1982

MANY VOLUMES HAVE been written about the world outside of us: the environment, society, politics, economics, and so on, but very few have gone to the length of discovering what we actually are, why human beings behave as they do—killing each other; following some authority, or some book, some person, some ideal; and having no right relationship with their friends, their wives, their husbands, and their children. Why have human beings become so vulgar, so brutal, utterly lacking in care for others, and denying the whole process of what is considered love?

And man has lived with wars for thousands of years. We are trying to stop nuclear war, but we will never stop wars. These go on in the people being exploited, and the oppressor becoming the oppressed. This is the cycle of human existence with sorrow, loneliness, a great sense of depression, mounting anxiety, utter lack of security, and there is no relationship with society or with one's own intimate friends. No relationship without conflict, quarrels, and so on. This is the world in which we live—which I am sure you all know.

And throughout these millennia our brains have been conditioned by knowledge. Please don't reject or accept anything that the speaker says. Question it, doubt it, be sceptical. Above all don't be influenced by the speaker, because we are so easily influenced, so gullible. And if we are to talk seriously about these matters, one must have a mind and a brain that are free to examine, free from bias, from any conclusion, from any opinion or obstinacy. One must have a brain that is constantly inquiring, doubting. It is only then that we can have a relationship with each other and so communicate.

Ojai, 22 May 1983

BE AWARE OF the beauty of every day, every fresh morning, the wonder of the world; it's a marvellous world, and we are destroying it, in our relationship with each other and in our relationship to nature, to all the living things of this earth.

❖

CAN WE INQUIRE into what is a brain that is silent? It's only through great silence that you learn, you observe, not when you are making a lot of noise. To observe those hills, and these beautiful trees, to observe your family and friends, you must have space and there must be silence. But if you are chattering, gossiping, you have no space or silence. And we need space, not only physically, but much more psychologically. That space is denied when we are thinking about ourselves. It's so simple. Because when there is space, vast space psychologically, there is great vitality. But when that space is limited to one's own little self, that vast energy is totally contained with its limitation. So that's why meditation is the ending of self.

One can listen to all this endlessly, but if you don't do this, what is the point of your listening? If you actually are not aware of yourself, of your words, your gestures, your walk, the way you eat, why you drink and smoke, and all the rest of the things human beings are doing—if you are not aware of all the physical things, how can you be aware of what is going on profoundly?

If one is not aware, then one becomes shoddy, middle-class, mediocre. The root meaning of that word *mediocre* is "going half-way up the hill," going halfway up the mountain, never reaching the top of it. That's mediocrity. That is, never demanding of ourselves excellence, never demanding of ourselves total goodness or complete freedom—not freedom to do what we like, that is not freedom, that is triviality, but to be free from all pain of anxieties, loneliness, despair, and all the rest of it.

So to find out, or to come upon that, or for that to exist there must be great space and silence—not contrived silence, not thought saying, I must be silent. Silence is something extraordinary, it's not the silence between two noises. Peace is not between two wars. Silence is something that comes naturally when you are watching, when you are watching without motive, without any kind of demand, just to watch, and see the beauty of a single star in the sky, or to watch a single tree in a field, or to watch your wife or husband, or whatever you watch. To watch with a great silence and space. Then in that watching, in that alertness, there is something that is beyond words, beyond all measure.

We use words to measure the immeasurable. So one must be aware also of the network of words, how words cheat us, how words mean so much: *communism*, to a capitalist, means something terrible. Words become extraordinarily important. But to be aware of those words and to live with the word *silence*, knowing that the word is not silence, but to live with that word and see the weight of that word, the content of that word, the beauty of that word! So one begins to realize, when thought is quiet, watching, that there is something beyond all imagination, doubt, and seeking. And there is such a thing—at least for the speaker. But what the speaker says has no validity to another. If you listen, learn, watch, be totally free from all the anxieties of life, then only is there a religion that brings about a new, totally different culture. We are not cultured people at all. You may be very clever in business, you may be extraordinarily capable technologically, be a doctor or a professor; but we are still very limited.

The ending of the self, the "me": to be nothing. The word *nothing* means "not a thing." Not a thing created by thought. To be nothing; having no image of yourself. But we have a great many images of ourselves. To have no image of any kind, no illusion, to be absolutely nothing. The tree is nothing to itself. It exists. And in its very existence it is the most beautiful thing, like those hills: they exist. They don't become something, because they can't. Like a seed of an apple tree, it is apple; it doesn't try to become the pear, or another fruit—it *is*. You understand? This is meditation. This is the ending of the search, and truth *is*.

Brockwood Park,
4 September 1983

WE NEVER LOOK at life as a tremendous movement, with a great depth, a vastness. We have reduced our life to such a shoddy little affair. And life is really the most sacred thing in existence. To kill somebody is the most irreligious horror—and to get angry, to be violent with somebody.

❖

WE NEVER SEE the world as a whole because we are so fragmented. We are so terribly limited, so petty. And we never have this feeling of wholeness, where the things of the sea, of the earth and the sky, nature, the universe, are part of us. Not imagined—you can go off in some kind of fanciful imagination and imagine that we are the universe, then you become cuckoo! But, if you break down this small, self-centred interest, and have nothing of that, then from there you can move infinitely.

Ojai, 24 May 1984

Questioner: How is one to live on this earth without harm or destruction to its beauty, without bringing suffering and death to others?

Krishnamurti: Have you ever asked this question? Actually? Not theoretically but actually put that question, faced it? Don't run away from it, don't explain that suffering is necessary, and all the rest of it, but look at it, confront it. Have you ever asked such a question? Not en masse, not to make a demonstration against some politician who wants to destroy a National Park, or this or that. To ask such a question, that means you are burning with it, it is something tremendously real, not just a fanciful question to pass the time of day. To live on this earth with its extraordinary beauty, and not to destroy it; to end sorrow, and not kill another human being, not kill a living thing. There is a certain sect in India whose transportation is to walk; they take no trains, no airplanes, no carriages, and they put on a mask so as not to kill an insect by breathing. Some of that group came to see the speaker and they walked eight hundred miles. And they won't kill.

And there are those who kill: kill for sport, kill for amusement, kill for profit—the whole meat industry. Those who destroy the earth, dump poisonous gas, pollute the air, the waters, and pollute each other. This is what we are doing to the earth and to ourselves.

Can we live on this earth with its great beauty and not bring suffering or death to others? It is a very, very serious question. To live a life without causing suffering or death to others; that means not killing a human being, also not killing any animal for sport, or for your food. You understand all this? This is the question.

There was a certain class of people in India who never ate meat. They thought killing was wrong. They were called at the time, Brahmins. And western civilization has never inquired into whether killing is right, whether killing any living thing is justified. The western world has destroyed whole races of people. Right? America has destroyed the Indians, wiped them out because they wanted their land, and all that. So can we live on this earth without killing, without war? I can answer it, but then what value has it to you if you are killing? I am not advocating vegetarianism. (An author wrote some time ago: "Vegetarianism is spreading like some foul disease in this country"!) But you kill a cabbage, so where do you draw the line? Do you make a problem of it? Do you understand my question?

If you are against war, as certain human beings, including myself, are against war, killing other human beings for whatever reason, then you cannot post a letter! The stamp you buy, the food you get, part of what you pay goes to defence, armaments. If you buy petrol (gas in this country) part of that cost goes to it, and so on and so on. So what will you do? If you don't pay taxes you are fined or sent to jail. If you don't buy stamps or gas you can't write letters, you can't travel. So you drive yourself into a corner. And living in a corner seems rather futile. So what will you do? Do you say, "I won't travel, I won't write a letter"? All this helps to maintain the army and navy, and armaments—you follow—the whole racket of it. Or would you approach it differently? Why do we kill? Religions, especially Christianity, have killed very many people;

they have tortured people, called them heretics, burnt them. You know all the history of it. Also the Moslems have done it. Probably the Hindus and the Buddhists are the only people who have not killed—their religions forbid it.

How can one live on this earth without killing another and causing suffering for another? To go into this question really deeply is a very, very serious process. Is there that quality of love that answers this question? If you love another human being, are you willing to kill that person? Would you then kill anything, except that you need certain food, vegetables, nuts and so on, but, apart from that, would you kill anything? Go into all these questions, and live it, for god's sake, don't just talk about it.

What is dividing the world is ideals, the ideology of one group against another, this apparently everlasting division between man, woman, and so on. They have tried to bridge this through logic, through reason, through various institutions and foundations and organizations, and they have not succeeded in any way. This is a fact. Knowledge has not solved this problem either—knowledge in the sense of accumulated experience and so on. And thought has certainly not solved this problem.

So there is only one issue out of it: to discover what is love. Love is not desire, love is not possession, love is not selfish, egocentric activity—me first and you second. But apparently that love has no meaning to most people. They may write books about it, but it has no meaning, so they try to invent that quality, that perfume, that fire, that compassion. And compassion has its intelligence, that is supreme intelligence. When there is that intelligence, which is born of compassion, love, then all these problems will be solved simply, quietly. But we never pursue the question to the very end. We may pursue it intellectually, verbally, but if you do it with your heart, with your mind, with your passion behind it, then the earth will remain beautiful. And then there is a great sense of beauty in oneself.

From Krishnamurti's Journal, 4 April 1975

IF YOU LOSE TOUCH with nature you lose touch with humanity. If there's no relationship with nature then you become a killer; then you kill baby seals, whales, dolphins, and man either for gain, for "sport," for food, or for knowledge. Then nature is frightened of you, withdrawing its beauty. You may take long walks in the woods or camp in lovely places, but you are a killer and so lose their friendship. You probably are not related to anything, to your wife or your husband; you are much too busy, gaining and losing, with your own private thoughts, pleasures and pains. You live in your own dark isolation, and the escape from it is further darkness. Your interest is in a short survival, mindless, easygoing or violent. And thousands die of hunger or are butchered because of your irresponsibility. You leave the ordering of the world to the lying, corrupt politician, to the intellectuals, to the experts. Because you have no integrity, you build a society that's immoral, dishonest, a society based on utter selfishness. And then you escape from all this for which you alone are responsible, to the beaches, to the woods or carry a gun for "sport."

You may know all this, but knowledge does not bring about transformation in you. When you have this sense of the whole, you will be related to the universe.

Rajghat, 12 November 1984

To HAVE A religious mind the first demand or necessity is beauty. Beauty is not in a particular form—a beautiful face, a beautiful way of living, and so on. What is beauty? Without that there is no truth, there is no love; without beauty there is no sense of morality. Beauty in itself is virtue. Now, we are going to inquire together what is beauty. The speaker may put it into words, but you have to take the responsibility of inquiring for yourself what beauty is. Is beauty in a painting, the marvellous old sculptures of the Egyptians, the Greeks, or the Mahesha Murthi of Bombay, and so on? What is beauty? What does it mean to you? Is it the dress with the beautiful patterns of a sari, or the beautiful sky in the evening or early in the morning, the beauty of the mountain, the fields, and the valleys, the meadows, and the streams, the beauty of a bird, or the marvellous old trees? So does beauty depend on a particular culture or a particular tradition? The weavers of India have a tradition; they produce marvellous clothes and designs. Is that beauty? Or is beauty something totally different. When you observe great mountains with the eternal snows and deep valleys, the outlines of a magnificent, majestic mountain against a blue sky, when you perceive that for the first time or the hundredth time, what actually takes place?

What takes place when you see the river in the morning light with the sun just coming up and making a golden path along the waters? When you look at it, what takes place? Are you repeating some mantra, or for the moment are you completely silent? The beauty of that light on the water pushes aside all your problems, all your anxieties, everything else for a few seconds or a few minutes or for an hour, which means the self is not there: the self, the egoistic, self-centred activity, the self-interest. All that is banished by the great beauty of a cloud full of light and dignity—at that moment the self is absent. So, does not beauty exist when the self is not? Don't agree with it or nod your head and say, "He's quite right, how marvellous," and then go on with your selfishness and self-concern and talk logistically or theoretically about beauty. Beauty is something that must be perceived, not held in the mind as a remembrance. So, beauty is something far deeper, much more profound and extensive than a mere picture, a design, a beautiful face, or graceful manners. There is beauty only when the self is not. And that is the first thing that is required in understanding what is a religious mind.

And also inquiring into it must be a global brain, not a provincial, sectarian, limited brain. It must understand the vast human, complex problem. That is, a holistic mind, a brain that comprehends the whole of existence. Not your particular existence, your particular problems, because everywhere you go, whether in America, Europe, India, or Asia, we human beings suffer. . . . We are lonely, anxious, fearful, seeking comfort, unhappy, depressed, irritated, with occasional joy, pleasure, and so on.

A brain that is holistic is concerned with the whole of humanity, because we are all alike. And also we must find out for ourselves what is the relationship between nature and each of us. That is part of religion. You may not agree, but consider it, go into it. Have you any relationship with nature, with the birds, with the water of that river? All rivers are holy, but getting more and more polluted: you may call it Ganges, or the Thames, the Nile, the Rhine, the Mississippi, or the Volga. What is your relationship with all that—with the trees, with the birds, with all the living things that we call nature? Aren't we part of all that? So aren't we the environment? I wonder if I am talking nonsense, and you are just listening casually. Does it mean anything to you—all this—or am I a stranger from Mars talking about something with which you are not really related at all. Does it mean anything? It is up to you.

Madras, 29 December 1979

We are having a conversation about the nature of the mind and its extraordinary capacities. And we human beings through millennia after millennia have reduced this capacity to a very narrow, limited field. This vast energy of the mind has created technologically astonishing things. People have been to the moon, under the sea, and they have invented the most diabolical things. They have also brought about great benefits such as surgery and medicine. But this vast energy has been curtailed, limited, narrowed down and our lives are basically, if one observes closely, a field of struggle, a field of conflict, an area in which human beings are against each other, destroying each other; they have not only destroyed human beings, but they are also exploiting the earth and the seas. The word *exploit* means to use another for one's own profit. This exploitation goes on in every field of life.

And one wonders why human beings live the way we are living—the battle, the conflict, the confusion, the utter misery and sorrow; pleasure, and joys that soon fade away. We are left empty-handed, bitter, cynical, not believing in a thing, or we turn to tradition. But even that tradition is now losing its grip, and if you observe very closely the mind is now living not only physically but much more psychologically on commentaries, books, scriptures, the Bible, and the Koran. What happens to a mind that lives on books, not only in the schools, colleges, and universities, but also religiously? I am using the word *religious* in the ordinary sense of the word. When one lives by the book, one lives by words, by theories about what other people have said. And when one lives in that fashion, degeneration obviously must take place. You go back to the book, as the organized religions are doing, and use that as authority—brutal, dogmatic, cruel, and destructive. You live by the book, what other people have said, which you have accepted—the commentaries, and the commentaries on commentaries, and so on and so on and so on! And when faced with crises, this civilization, which has possibly existed for three thousand years or more, collapses. Degeneration takes place, corruption at all levels of life—the industrialized gurus, the politicians, the businessmen, the religious people—the whole thing is collapsing.

One has asked various people what is the cause of this decay, this degeneration, and they have really no answer. They give you examples of degeneration, but although one has discussed with various pundits, scholars, and professors, they do not seem to find the root of this decay. I do not know if you have thought about it. If you have given serious thought to it, would it be true to say that you have lived on other people's ideas, other people's doctrines, other people's beliefs? And so the result, apparently, is that when one lives a secondhand life—a life based on words, ideas, beliefs—your mind, the totality of the mind, naturally withers.

We mean by that word *mind*, all the active senses with their neurological reactions, all the emotions, all the desires, the technological knowledge, and the cultivation of memory, which is the capacity to think clearly or confusedly. This mind has been seeking that germ which man has planted from the beginning of time, which has never flowered, that seed of real religiosity. Because without that kind of religion there can be no new civilization, no new culture. There may be new systems, new philosophies, new social structures; but it will be the same pattern repeated over and over and over again.

So what shall we do? You, as a human being living on this marvellous earth with the beauteous mountains and landscapes, and the seas and the waters . . . which is not poetic, I am just pointing it out. What can we do together to break through? That is, not to create new systems; new social systems; new religious orders; new sets of beliefs, ideals, and dogmas; and new rituals, because that game has been played over and over and over again. To bring about a different world, if you are at all serious, the quality of goodness has to come into being. The word *good* means to be whole, not broken up, not fragmented; a human being who is good implies there is no sense of division. He is in himself complete, whole, without any sense of conflict.

We are exploring together the thing that is our present crisis—not merely economic, social, but the crisis in our consciousness, in our very being, not the crisis of a new system, not the crisis of war and so on. It is a crisis in the very being of humanity. And in what manner can this consciousness be transformed?

What will make you change? A crisis? A knock on the head? Sorrow? Tears? All that has happened, in crisis after crisis. We have shed tears endlessly and nothing seems to change man because you are relying on somebody else to do the job: your masters, your gurus, your books, your professors, your clever cunning people who have new theories. Nobody says, "I am going to find out." Although the whole history of mankind is in us, we never read our own book! It is all there, but we never take the trouble, or have the patience and the persistent inquiry. We prefer to live in this chaos, in this misery.

So, what will make you change? Please ask yourself, burn with that question, because we have fallen into habit. Your house is burning, and apparently you do not pay attention. So, if you don't change, society remains as it is. And clever people are coming along saying that society must change, which means a new structure, and the structure then becomes more important than man, as all revolutions have shown.

After considering all this, is there a learning, is there an awakening of intelligence, is there a sense of order in our lives, or are we going back to the same routine? If you have that intelligence, that goodness, that sense of great love, then you will create a marvellous new society where we can all live happily. It's our earth, not Indian earth, or English earth, or Russian earth; it's our earth where we can live happily, intelligently, not at each other's throats. So, please give your heart and mind to find out why you don't change—even in little things. Please pay attention to your own life. You have extraordinary capacities. It is all waiting for you to open the door.

From Krishnamurti's Notebook, *24 October 1961*

THE MOON WAS just coming over the hills, caught in a long serpentine cloud, giving her a fantastic shape. She was huge, dwarfing the hills, the earth, and the green pastures; where she was coming up was more clear, fewer clouds, but she soon disappeared in dark rain-bearing clouds. It began to drizzle and the earth was glad; it doesn't rain much here and every drop counts. The big banyan and the tamarind and the mango would struggle through, but the little plants and the rice crop were rejoicing at even a little rain. Unfortunately even the few drops stopped and presently the moon shone in a clear sky. It was raining furiously on the coast, but here where the rain was needed, the rain-bearing clouds passed away. It was a beautiful evening, and there were deep dark shadows of many patterns. The moon was very bright and the shadows were very still and the leaves, washed clean, were sparkling. Walking and talking, meditation was going on below the words and the beauty of the night. It was going on at a great depth, flowing outwardly and inwardly; it was exploding and expanding. One was aware of it; it was happening; one wasn't experiencing it, experiencing is limiting; it was taking place. There was no participation in it; thought could not share it for thought is such a futile and mechanical thing anyhow, nor could emotion get entangled with it; it was too disturbingly active for either. It was happening at such an unknown depth for which there was no measurement. But there was great stillness. It was quite surprising and not at all ordinary.

The dark leaves were shining and the moon had climbed quite high; she was on the westerly course and flooding the room. Dawn was many hours away and there was not a sound, even the village dogs, with their shrill yapping, were quiet. Waking, it was there, with clarity and precision; the otherness was there and waking up was necessary, not sleep. It was deliberate, to be aware of what was happening, to be aware with full consciousness of what was taking place.

Asleep, it might have been a dream, a hint of the unconscious, a trick of the brain, but fully awake, this strange and unknowable otherness was a palpable reality, a fact and not an illusion, a dream. It had a quality, if such a word can be applied to it, of weightlessness and impenetrable strength. Again these words have certain significance, definite and communicable, but these words lose all their meaning when the otherness has to be conveyed in words; words are symbols, but no symbol can ever convey the reality. It was there with such incorruptible strength that nothing could destroy it, for it was unapproachable. You can approach something with which you are familiar, you must have the same language to commune, some kind of thought process, verbal or non-verbal; above all there must be mutual recognition. There was none. On your side you may say it is this or that, this or that quality, but at the moment of the happening there was no verbalization for the brain was utterly still, without any movement of thought. But the otherness is without relationship to anything and all thought and being is a cause-effect process, and so there was no understanding of it or relationship with it. It was an unapproachable flame and you could only look at it and keep your distance. And on waking suddenly, it was there. And with it came unexpected ecstasy, an unreasonable joy; there was no cause for it for it has never been sought or pursued. There was this ecstasy on waking again at the usual hour; it was there and continued for a lengthy period of time.

25 October

There is a long-stemmed weed, grass of some kind, which grows wildly in the garden, and it has a feathery flowering, burnt gold, flashing in the breeze, swaying till it almost breaks but never breaking, except in a strong wind. There is a clump of these weeds of golden beige, and when the breeze blows it sets them dancing; each stem has its own rhythm, its own splendour, and they are like a wave when they all move together. The colour then, with the evening light, is indescribable; it is the colour of the sunset, of the earth, and of the golden hills and clouds. The flowers beside them were too definite, too crude, demanding that you look at them. These weeds had a strange delicacy; they had a faint smell of wheat and of ancient times; they were sturdy and pure, full of abundant life. An evening cloud was passing by, full of light as the sun went down behind the dark hill. The rain had given to the earth a goodly smell, and the air was pleasantly cool. The rains were coming and there was hope in the land.

Of a sudden it happened, coming back to the room; it was there with an embracing welcome, so unexpected. One had come in only to go out again; we had been talking about several things, nothing too serious. It was a shock and a surprise to find this welcoming otherness in the room; it was waiting there with such open invitation that an apology seemed futile. Several times, on the Common, [Wimbledon Common. He was remembering London where he had stayed in May in a house at Wimbledon.] far away from here under some trees, along a path that was used by so many, it would be waiting just as the path turned; with astonishment one stood there, near those trees, completely open, vulnerable, speechless, without a movement. It was not a fancy, a self-projected delusion; the other, who happened to be there, felt it too. On several occasions it was there, with an all-embracing welcome of love, and it was quite incredible. Every time it had a new quality, a new beauty, a new austerity. And it was like that in this room, something totally new and wholly unexpected. It was beauty that made the entire mind still and the body without a movement;

it made the mind, the brain and the body intensely alert and sensitive; it made the body tremble and in a few minutes that welcoming otherness was gone, as swiftly as it must have come. No thought or fanciful emotion could ever conjure up such a happening. Thought is petty, do what it will, and feeling is so fragile and deceitful; neither of them, in their wildest endeavour could build up these happenings. They are too immeasurably great, too immense in their strength and purity for thought or feeling; these have roots and they have none. They are not to be invited or held; thought-feeling can play every kind of clever and fanciful trick, but they cannot invent or contain the otherness. It is by itself and nothing can touch it.

28 October

There is a red flower among the dark green leaves and from the verandah you only see that. There are the hills, the red sand of the riverbeds, the big high banyan tree, and the many tamarinds, but you only see that flower, it is so gay, so full of colour. There is no other colour; the patches of blue sky, the burning clouds of light, the violet hills, the rich green of the rice field, all these fade away and only this wondrous colour of that flower remains. It fills the whole sky and the valley; it will fade and fall away; it will cease and the hills will endure. But this morning it was eternity, beyond all time and thought; it held all love and joy; there was no sentiment and romantic absurdities in it, nor was it a symbol of something else. It was itself, to die in the evening, but it contained all life. It was not something you reasoned out nor was it a thing of unreason, some romantic fancy; it was as actual as those hills and those voices calling to each other. It was the complete meditation of life, and illusion exists only when the impact of fact ceases. That cloud so full of light is a reality whose beauty has no furious impact on a mind that is made dull and insensitive by influence, habit, and the everlasting search for security. Security in fame, in relationship, in knowledge destroys sensitivity and deterioration sets in. That flower, those hills and the blue restless sea are the challenge, as nuclear bombs, of life, and only the sensitive mind can respond to them totally; only a total response leaves no marks of conflict, and conflict indicates partial response.

The so-called saints and sannyasis have contributed to the dullness of mind and to the destruction of sensitivity. Every habit, repetition, ritual strengthened by belief and dogma, sensory response, can be and are refined, but the alert awareness, sensitivity, is quite another matter. Sensitivity is absolutely essential to look deeply within. This movement of going within is not a reaction to the outer; the outer and the inner are the same movement—they are not separate. The division of this movement as the outer and as the inner breeds insensitivity. Going within is the natural flow of the outer; the movement of the inner has its own action, expressed outwardly but it is not a reaction of the outer. Awareness of this whole movement is sensitivity.

31 October

It was a beautiful evening: the air was clean, the hills were blue, violet, and dark purple; the rice fields had plenty of water and were a varying rich green from light to metallic to dark flashing green; some trees had already withdrawn for the night, dark and silent and others were still open and held the light of day. The clouds were black over the western hills, and to the north and east the clouds were full of the reflection of the evening sun, which had set behind the heavy purple hills. There was no one on the road, the few that passed were silent and there wasn't a patch of blue sky, clouds were gathering in for the night. Yet everything seemed to be awake, the rocks, the dry riverbed, the bushes in the fading light. Meditation, along that quiet and deserted road came like a soft rain over the hills; it came as easily and naturally as the coming night. There was no effort of any kind and no control with its concentrations and distractions; there was no order and pursuit, no denial or acceptance, nor any continuity of memory in meditation. The brain was aware of its environment but quiet without response, uninfluenced but recognizing without responding. It was very quiet and words had faded with thought. There was that strange energy—call it by any other name, it has no importance whatsoever—deeply active, without object and purpose; it was creation, without the canvas and the marble, and destructive; it was not the thing of human brain, of expression and decay. It was not approachable, to be classified and analysed, and thought and feeling are not the instruments of its comprehension. It was completely unrelated to everything and totally alone in its vastness and immensity. And walking along that darkening road, there was the ecstasy of the impossible, not of achievement, arriving, success, and all those immature demands and responses, but the aloneness of the impossible. The possible is mechanical and the impossible can be envisaged, tried, and perhaps achieved, which in turn becomes mechanical. But the ecstasy had no cause, no reason. It was simply there, not as an experience but as a fact, not to be accepted or denied, to be argued over and dissected. It was not a thing to be sought after, for there is no path to it. Everything has to die for it to be, death, destruction, which is love.

A poor, worn-out labourer, in torn dirty clothes, was returning home with his bone-thin cow.

2 November

It had become very cloudy, all the hills were heavy with them and clouds were piling up in every direction. It was spitting with rain and there wasn't a blue patch anywhere; the sun had set in darkness, and the trees were aloof and distant. There is an old palm tree that stood out against the darkening sky and whatever light there was was held by it. The riverbeds were silent, their red sand moist, but there was no song; the birds had become silent taking shelter among the thick leaves. A breeze was blowing from the northeast and with it came more dark clouds and a spattering of rain, but it hadn't begun in earnest; that would come later in gathering fury. And the road in front was empty; it was red, rough, and sandy and the dark hills looked down on it. It was a pleasant road with hardly any cars and the villagers with their ox-drawn carts going from one village to another. The villagers were dirty, skeleton-thin, in rags, and their stomachs drawn in, but they were wiry and enduring; they had lived like that for centuries and no government is going to change all this overnight. But these people had a smile, though their eyes were weary. They could dance after a heavy day's labour and they had fire in them, they were not hopelessly beaten down. The land had not had good rains for many years and this may be one of those fortunate years that may bring more food for them and fodder for their thin cattle. And the road went on and joined at the mouth of the valley the big road with few buses and cars. And on this road, far away were the cities with their filth, industries, rich houses, temples, and dull minds. But here on this open road, there was solitude and the many hills, full of age and indifference.

❖

AND WALKING ON that road there was complete emptiness of the brain, and the mind was free of all experience, the knowing of yesterday, though a thousand yesterdays have been. Time, the thing of thought, had stopped; literally there was no movement before and after; there was no going or arriving or standing still. Space as distance was not; there were the hills and bushes but not as high and low. There was no relationship with anything, but there was an awareness of the bridge and the passer-by. The totality of the mind, in which is the brain with its thoughts and feelings, was empty; and because it was empty, there was energy, a deepening and widening energy without measure. All comparison, measurement belong to thought and so to time. The otherness was the mind without time; it was the breath of innocence and immensity. Words are not reality; they are only means of communication, but they are not the innocence and the immeasurable. The emptiness was alone.

Sources and Acknowledgments

From the Verbatim Report of the eighth public talk in Poona, 17 October 1948, in *Collected Works of J. Krishnamurti*, copyright © 1991 Krishnamurti Foundation of America.

From the Verbatim Report of the first public talk in New Delhi, 14 November 1948, in *Collected Works of J. Krishnamurti*, copyright © 1991 Krishnamurti Foundation of America.

From *From Darkness to Light*, copyright © 1980 K. & R. Foundation.

From *Krishnamurti's Journal*, 6 April 1975, copyright © 1982 Krishnamurti Foundation Trust, Ltd.

From the Verbatim Report of the second public talk in New Delhi, 28 November 1948, in *Collected Works of J. Krishnamurti*, copyright © 1991 Krishnamurti Foundation of America.

From the Verbatim Report of the second public talk in Varanasi, 22 November 1964, in *Collected Works of J. Krishnamurti*, copyright © 1991 Krishnamurti Foundation of America.

From the Verbatim Report of the fifth public talk in Varanasi, 28 November 1964, in *Collected Works of J. Krishnamurti*, copyright © 1991 Krishnamurti Foundation of America.

From *Commentaries on Living, Second Series*, copyright © 1958 Krishnamurti Writings, Inc.

From *The First and Last Freedom*, chapter 3, copyright © 1954 Krishnamurti Writings, Inc.